D1646504

UNIVERSITY OF

Autism, Discrimination and the Law

KA 0305033 5

of related interest

Disabled Children and the Law
Research and Good Practice 2nd edition
Janet Read, Luke Clements and David Ruebain
ISBN: 978 1 84310 280 9

Law, Rights and Disability
Edited by Jeremy Cooper
ISBN 978 1 85302 836 6

Access and Inclusion for Children with Autistic Spectrum Disorders
'Let Me In'
Matthew Hesmondhalgh and Christine Breakey
ISBN 978 1 85302 986 8

The Nearest Relative Handbook
David Hewitt
ISBN 978 1 84310 522 0

Surviving the Special Educational Needs System
How to be a 'Velvet Bulldozer' (DVD)
Sandy Row
ISBN 978 1 84310 262 5

Community Care Practice and the Law
Third Edition
Michael Mandelstam
ISBN 978 1 85302 750 5

Autism, Discrimination and the Law

A Quick Guide for Parents, Educators and Employers

James Graham

Jessica Kingsley Publishers
London and Philadelphia

UNIVERSITY OF WINCHESTER
LIBRARY

First published in 2008
by Jessica Kingsley Publishers
116 Pentonville Road
London N1 9JB, UK
and
400 Market Street, Suite 400
Philadelphia, PA 19106, USA

www.jkp.com

Copyright © James Graham 2008

All rights reserved. No part of this publication may be reproduced in any material form (including photocopying or storing it in any medium by electronic means and whether or not transiently or incidentally to some other use of this publication) without the written permission of the copyright owner except in accordance with the provisions of the Copyright, Designs and Patents Act 1988 or under the terms of a licence issued by the Copyright Licensing Agency Ltd, Saffron House, 6–10 Kirby Street, London EC1N 8TS. Applications for the copyright owner's written permission to reproduce any part of this publication should be addressed to the publisher.

Warning: The doing of an unauthorised act in relation to a copyright work may result in both a civil claim for damages and criminal prosecution.

Library of Congress Cataloging in Publication Data

Graham, James.
Autism, discrimination, and the law : a quick guide for parents, educators, and employers / James Graham.
p. cm.
Includes bibliographical references and index.
ISBN 978-1-84310-627-2 (pb : alk. paper) 1. Discrimination against people with disabilities--Law and legislation. 2. People with disabilities--Legal status, laws, etc. 3. People with disabilities--Civil rights. 4. Autism. I. Title.
K637.G73 2008
342.7308'7--dc22
2007033855

British Library Cataloguing in Publication Data
A CIP catalogue record for this book is available from the British Library

ISBN 978 1 84310 627 2

Printed and bound in Great Britain by
Athenaeum Press, Gateshead, Tyne and Wear

UNIVERSITY OF WINCHESTER

03050335

Contents

Preface

People with autism are different from people with other types of impairments. People with autism have impairments in their social abilities. If you do not ensure that people with autism are treated as favourably as others in any of the services you provide – in the same way that you will have adapted to people with physical impairments – you can now be the subject of a legal claim where a person with autism, or their representative, can seek a declaration that they have been discriminated against and awarded compensation for any injury to feelings that has resulted from that discrimination.

You can get a feel for an emerging picture of litigation simply by looking in the various magazines for special needs groups to note the increasing numbers of lawyers advertising their services.

Written for the widest possible audience and in an accessible style, this book will enable you to identify, plan for and provide *reasonable adjustments* to people with autism who may use your services and will enable others to consider if they are being discriminated against.

Disclaimer

This book is intended to provide guidance on the law as it relates to disability discrimination. It is not a comprehensive guide and it is not intended to be a substitute for legal advice on a specific case.

Acknowledgements

Considerable thanks must be extended to Nicholas Graham, Assistant Head of Legal Services at Oxfordshire County Council and principal adviser on education and disability issues, who wrote Chapters 2 and 5, and to Nicola Leonard, Head of Education at The INTERACT Centre and now working for the careers service, and Karen Reeves, a specialist speech and language therapist (advanced) at the National Autistic Society's Sybil Elgar School in London, who both read and advised me on the manuscript.

A note of thanks also to Helen Graham, Christina Graham (Mum) and the capabilities, expertise and teaching abilities of Harriet Fisher, Glen Reddick, Mark Deane, Kira Brabenec, and of Richard Davies and Ben Kaye.

Introduction

A whole industry of support services, university courses, books and research groups has grown up around the emergence of people with disabilities. Many of the people in support services spend a great deal of time looking at ways that they can help people with disabilities, such as those that have autism, fit in and be included. Many have relied on ideas of 'inclusion' and use words like 'should' and 'deserve' and 'committed to'. These words are used to demonstrate how people with autism *should* have the same access to goods and services as others and *should not* be excluded from education, employment and a companionable life.

Some people within these support services try to persuade people with autism that it is they who need to change by teaching them 'social skills' – the very things in which they are impaired. How often have you seen written on a statement of special educational needs that a person with autism has 'problems concentrating in class' or 'poor relationships with peers' and therefore needs to be taught how to concentrate or have his or her social skills improved? How many of you have counselled people with autism who have almost gone mad having been supported to try to learn things and take part in social exchanges that they were told they would be able to do and yet do not have the mental faculties to do them? How many times have you read that people with autism need to develop or learn 'coping strategies' – as if they do not have enough to deal with when coping with other people and making sense of the world around them, they now have to be able to cope with themselves. And how many people with autism do you know who have not been able to take part in lessons, employment or the same activities as their peers simply because they have autism?

The Office for Standards in Education, Children's Services and Skills (Ofsted) reported that:

> Not enough use is made by mainstream schools of the potential for adapting the curriculum and teaching methods so that pupils have suitable opportunities to improve key skills.
>
> Over half the schools visited had no disability access plans and, of those plans that did exist, the majority focused only on accommodation. (Ofsted 2004, p.5)

This lack of adaptation and the over-focus on the environment could be seen as discrimination where pupils with autism are concerned. In 2006 there was a great deal of criticism of the policy of inclusion and how forcing people into settings could be a 'form of abuse' (Education Guardian 2006).

In September 2006, the Children's Commissioner for England, Professor Sir Al Aynsley-Green, said that it was 'shameful' that the UK was failing to provide adequately for children with autism. He said in a BBC interview that:

> It's appalling and it's shameful for our country, the fifth richest economy in the world, to have so many children that are not being looked after and given the resources they need to develop to their full potential. (BBC 2006)

Changes in the law

There is now a law, the Disability Discrimination Act 1995, which makes it illegal to discriminate against people on the basis of their disabilities. People who provide services of any sort have to make adjustments to those services to prevent people from being discriminated against.

> Among the services which are covered [by the discrimination law] are those provided to the public by local councils, Government departments and agencies, the emergency services, charities, voluntary organisations, hotels, restaurants, pubs, post offices, banks, building societies, solicitors, accountants, telecommunications and broadcasting organisations, public utilities (such as gas, electricity and water suppliers), national parks, rts stadia, leisure centres, advice agencies, theatres, cinemas, hairsers, shops, market stalls, petrol stations, telesales businesses, places

of worship, courts, hospitals and clinics. (Disability Discrimation Act 1995, Code of Practice 'Rights of Access Goods, Facilities, Services and Premises' from www.equalityhumanrights.com. Disability Rights Commission 2002, s19(3), para. 2.14, p.8)

This means that people with disabilities can no longer expect just to be included: the service must adapt to the person with the disability by making *reasonable adjustments.*

It is no longer about support and ideas of inclusion, it's about the law.

In relation to people with autism, it could be considered discriminatory if schools, colleges, employers and public bodies fail to

- provide opportunities to demonstrate through practice, on the job

- provide a host to navigate the pre-entry and admissions processes

- provide materials and information in a manner that the person can understand

- make adaptations to communications

- provide time to acclimatise to other people and situations

- provide help to manage and acclimatise to new tasks

- provide explicit information and explanation, signposts etc.

- provide opportunities to rehearse and practice

- provide managed transition arrangements

- give clear and explicit expectations and rules.

You can probably think of others.

What is this book about?

This book is *not* about 'interventions' or 'educational strategies', nor is it about 'treatment'. This book is about the *legal duties* that people have toward people with autism and the need to change or adapt processes and procedures in order to avoid discrimination when compared to other people in the same setting.

Chapter 1

This chapter is primarily geared to those who know little about the subject and acts a refresher for those who think they do. We look at issues of 'impairment' and 'disability' and introduce four concepts about the impairment that is autism:

- triad of impairments

- theory of mind

- central coherence

- executive function.

Chapter 1 also notes that the legal requirement to make reasonable adjustments implies that 'approaches' to people with autism that attempt to locate the 'problem' exclusively within the individual alone could also now be considered discriminatory.

Chapter 2

Written by Nicholas Graham, this chapter looks at the Disability Discrimination Act 1995. The Act is examined through the format of frequently asked questions (FAQs). The chapter explains the terminology used, such as *reasonable adjustments*, and examines as its backbone the case of Motorola versus Hewett: a situation where a man with autism successfully brought a case against his employer for 'less favourable treatment' and 'failures to make reasonable adjustments'.

The chapter looks at what discrimination amounts to and the problems faced by people with autism when much of the legislation is focused on physical impairments, and modern life is actually full of social and inter-personal demands.

Chapter 3

Bringing together Chapters 1 and 2, these case studies provide examples of discrimination against people with autism in three different settings:

- Antonio, a student with typical autism, who attended a general further education college

- Jonathon, a man with Asperger syndrome (a mild form of autism), who had a job in a local government office

- Janet, a young woman with autism and additional learning difficulties, who had just returned from a specialist residential college to a busy London day centre for people with general learning difficulties.

The case studies detail the problems that arose, how they related to their autism and what *reasonable adjustments* were made by the institutions and the people around them in order that the person with autism was not discriminated against. The case studies illustrate how difficult it is for many people with autism to be able to think about how other people might make adaptations for them and, when much of the focus is on physical impairments, adjustments to the social processes needed to occur. It also illustrates that if people with physical impairments are having *reasonable adjustments* made (e.g. level access ramps, signers), and people with social impairments such as autism are not, this amounts to discrimination.

The chapter looks at the general reasonable adjustments that schools and colleges and employers need to be making for people with autism.

Chapter 4

Chapter 4 mainly comprises a table that lists the problems that arise for people with autism, how they relate to the impairment of autism and what reasonable adjustments might be made.

Chapter 5

Nicholas Graham has written a guide to what you can do if you think you are discriminated against.

1

Autism

Introduction

There is a vast amount of information describing the nature of autism, which is usually written for people who already have a professional interest in the subject. This chapter is for people who have an interest in autism thrust upon them for one reason or another, professional or otherwise.

Autism was first described as a unique 'childhood disorder' in a paper published in 1943 by the American psychiatrist Leo Kanner. A year later Hans Asperger outlined a version of autism that became known as Asperger syndrome. Both autism and Asperger syndrome are complex developmental, genetic, neurobiological conditions that affect males more than females and are essentially impairments in the processes by which people relate to other people and the world around them.

Some facts

Since 1965 the numbers of people diagnosed as having autism have been on the increase. In 1979 it was estimated that there was an overall prevalence rate of 20 per 10,000 (Wing and Gould 1979). In 2005, a survey by the Office for National Statistics of the mental health of children and young people in the UK found a prevalence rate of 90 in 10,000 (Green *et al.* 2005). Gillian Baird and others surveyed a population of children aged between 9 and 10 years and her results indicate a prevalence of some 116 in 10,000 (Baird et al. 2006).

The UK National Autistic Society used 2001 Census information to give a best estimate of about 1 in every 100 people, which makes for a total of around 587,900 people having a form of autism in the UK.

Before we look at what autism is, we need to be clear about what we mean when we talk about 'impairment' and 'disability'. (There will be more on the meaning of disability as it relates to the law in Chapter 2.)

Disability

The Disability Discrimination Act 1995 (DDA) defines disability as:

> (1) Subject to the provisions of Schedule 1, a person has a disability for the purposes of this Act if he has a physical or mental impairment which has a substantial and long-term adverse effect on his ability to carry out normal day-to-day activities. (Disability Discrimination Act 1995 (c.50). Part one, section one)

> (2) In this Act 'disabled person' means a person who has a disability.

This is what is known as the 'medical model'. It locates the 'problem', the disability, within the individual. Many of the approaches to autism that you may have read about adopt the medical model, that is they suggest that the person with autism can be, indeed should be, 'cured', 'fixed' or 'taught' out of it. However:

> A person also discriminates against a disabled person if he fails to comply with a duty to make reasonable adjustments imposed on him in relation to the disabled person. (*ibid.*)

This requirement in the Act to make *reasonable adjustments* follows what is known as the 'social model' of disability. It locates the 'problem' that the person with disabilities has as a set of discriminatory barriers within a service, employment or process. (The case study of Motorola in Chapter 2 explores this issue further.)

The DDA implies that by making reasonable adjustments, the person with the impairment is no longer disabled.

> *The legal requirement to make reasonable adjustments implies that approaches to people with autism that attempt to locate the 'problem' exclusively within the individual alone could now be considered discriminatory.*

The idea of making reasonable adjustments chimes with what has become known as the 'social model of disability' (Oliver 1990). The social model argues that people with accredited or perceived impairments, regardless of cause, are disabled by society's failure to accommodate their needs ...'disability' is not a product of individual failings, but is socially created. (Barnes *et al.* 2002, p.5).

There is much debate about the effectiveness of the social model of disability and some have argued that the colonialism of the medical model has been hijacked and replaced by the colonialism of the sociological model.

In relation to the law and day-to-day life, what is useful about the social model is that it makes the distinction between *impairment* and *disability*. People with autistic conditions have *impairments* that can lead to *disabilities* in everyday functioning if people running services do not make reasonable adjustments when comparing them to members of the population using the same services.

In this chapter we are going to focus on *impairments,* on what people with autism cannot do and, while this is going to present a quite negative view, it is the only way to get a handle on the adaptations and adjustments others need to make for them.

What is autism?

Autism is much more complicated than most other 'impairments' – mental or physical. In 1943, Kanner concluded that the children he was studying 'have come into the world with innate inability to form the usual biologically provided affective contact with people, just as other children come into the world with innate physical or intellectual handicaps' (Frith 1989, p.9). Much has changed about our descriptions of autism since Kanner but it is this core feature, this difficulty in forming 'usual' relationships described by Kanner as an 'autistic aloneness', which remains in any diagnoses.

There are two main tools currently used by doctors, psychiatrists, psychologists and others for diagnosing someone as autistic: they are the World Health Organization's *International Classification of Diseases* (WHO 1992: ICD-10) and the American Psychiatric Association's *Diagnostic and Statistical Manual of Mental Disorders* (APA 1994: DSM-IV).

Autism has also been described as a *spectrum* or a *continuum* because there are degrees to which a person can have autism: from severe through to mild, often referred to as an Autistic Spectrum Disorder (ASD). Asperger syndrome has its differences from Kanner's autism (see Happé 1994) and its own entry in the ICD-10 and DSM-IV; it is commonly considered to be a 'mild' form of autism.

For the layperson, and for the purposes of this brief guidebook, there are four basic ideas about autism that it is useful to know:

- triad of impairment

- theory of mind

- central coherence

- executive function.

While these four areas of impairment relate and overlap, they will be dealt with separately. What will accumulate is a picture of characteristics that make up autism.

Triad of impairment

In 1979 Lorna Wing and Judith Gould (mentioned in the Introduction) carried out an epidemiological survey of all children living in an area of Camberwell in South London. Their study gave rise to what has become well known as autism's *triad of impairment*. These three impairments tie in closely with the diagnostic criteria outlined in the ICD-10 and DSM-IV.

There are three main impairments: social impairments, communication impairments and imagination impairments.

Social impairments

People with autism:

- can actively avoid eye contact and/or have awkward eye contact

- can behave as if other people do not exist (that is, not as usually understood)

- find it difficult to gauge what the other person might be feeling in a social interaction and/or not consider that the feelings they know about have a role to play during an interaction

- might not respond in ways that would be expected when they are spoken to
- may not always see themselves as part of or belonging to the social community or family group
- have difficulties in reading and using facial expressions and might be able to convey only intense pleasure, anger or anxiety
- are often unable to recognise emotional states in others
- may treat other people as objects in the environment and not as sentient beings
- may not respond to cuddles and affection from parents
- can sometimes be excessively polite and/or too formal in relating to other people
- can stick rigidly to the rules of a social interaction without the accompanying understanding
- may not seek comfort or ask for help from other people when distressed
- may not see other people as sources of help, support or comfort
- exhibit little or no play or engage in abnormal social play
- may often prefer solitary activities
- have (so-called) impaired peer relationships
- may lack understanding of how to make friends or the social conventions involved in being with other people
- may confuse the reciprocal nature of 'normal' interactions
- in the main, seem to be in a world of their own.

Communication

People with autism:

- may repeat words spoken to them (this is known as echolalia)

- may explain things or give answers in much greater detail than is necessary

- may reply to questions as if they were reading from a book, lacking inflection and drama

- may have word-finding problems, confusion over meaning of words and the sounds between words

- can be quite literal in interpreting phrases (e.g. the drinks are on the house or it's raining cats and dogs)

- may find humour and jokes difficult to grasp

- may have problems with the volume of their voices and can be too loud or too quiet

- may sound mechanical or robotic, their intonation may be odd, and pitch, intonation and stress awkward

- find that social communication in the use of body language, gestures, facial expressions, gait, posture or deportment can be misread and misused

- may fail to sustain or engage in conversation and may have a limited repertoire of 'conversational' topics

- may have difficulties in knowing what is *relevant* to talk about

- may fail to understand suggestions, warnings or teasing.

Imagination
What we mean here by imagination is the ability to 'think about'.
People with autism:

- can lack the facilities for creative play (although see Fitzgerald 2006)

- can have odd and repetitive body movements, such as flicking, twisting, spinning

- may have a persistent preoccupation with parts of the objects or toy and not the whole thing

- can have strong attachments to unusual objects

- may become distressed with what seem trivial changes in their environments

- can seem 'unreasonable' in their need to follow a particular routine in detail

- may have a significantly restricted range of interest or preoccupations with one 'narrow' interest

- can have impairments in their abilities to copy or imitate.

Summary

People with autism are said to have impairments in three main areas: in their social skills, their communication skills and in their imaginative abilities.

Theory of mind

One morning a boy called Jack is playing with his favourite toy truck when he has to leave for school. He puts his truck carefully away into his toy box. While he is at school his younger brother, Oscar, takes Jack's truck out of the toy box and plays with it in the garden. When Oscar finishes playing, he leaves the truck out in the garden. When Jack comes home from school, he wants to play with his truck. Where will he look for it?

We can be relatively sure that you know the answer to this question because you can think about what is going on in Jack's mind; you know what Jack is thinking. You know that Jack *believes* that the truck is in his toy box where he left it. Most children by the age of 4 years old can answer this question correctly and say that Jack will look in his toy box for the truck.

Reading other people's minds is something most of us can do without even thinking about it. Most of us know that other people have beliefs, desires, intentions, feelings, ideas, interests and motives different from our own and we can often tell, we can *read*, what these are. It is said that we have a *theory* about other people's minds.

UNIVERSITY OF WINCHESTER
LIBRARY

You know that Jack will look into his toy box with the *intention* of playing with his truck because he *believes* it is in there. You have the 'ability to predict relationships between external states of affairs and internal states of mind' (Frith 1989, pp.156–7).

People with autism have impairments in their *theory of mind*, in their ability to think about other people in the 'usual' ways. They find mind-reading difficult. This difficulty is sometimes referred to as 'mind-blindness' and it is linked to problems of 'pretending' and 'representing' (thinking about things).

In the example given at the beginning of this section, an autistic person will think that Jack will look for his truck in the garden. The autistic person will not be able to tell that he knows something different from Jack, something Jack doesn't know. The autistic person will think that because they know where Oscar has moved the truck, Jack knows.

Having a theory of mind allows you to think about your own thinking, it allows you to be self-conscious and reflect on your own behaviour and thoughts, to varying degrees. This in turn allows you to distinguish fiction from reality. Also, if you can imagine and think about yourself you can predict what you might do in a situation, you can choreograph yourself in a future event saying or doing something. You can also explain your own behaviours, and attribute motives and intentions to yourself. (Note that the inability to think about the mental states of others or of oneself may not be exclusive to autism.)

People with autism, and it should be borne in mind that this varies, find it hard to think about themselves and have problems telling fact from fiction. They find it hard to predict what they might do in a future situation and so understanding consequence is difficult. Related to this, they will find it hard to explain and think about their own behaviours. That people with autism have difficulties in thinking about and understanding other people's minds as well as their own is a significant impairment. The social world and other people are unpredictable, unreadable, terrifying sometimes, odd and often illogical.

The understanding of social interaction

Conversation, staying on topic, taking turns during an interaction, physical proximity, eye contact and so on: we take it for granted that these things will occur 'appropriately' in our everyday social lives. When we meet someone who has 'impairments' in these areas and who doesn't conform to expected ways of behaving in social situations – for example, standing too close, talking in a one-sided manner for a very long time, making inappropriate comments – it can generate a response that can lead us to ostracise that person.

For some people with autism, adhering to and understanding the rules, procedures and protocols of social interaction in everyday life is technically difficult, sometimes constitutionally impossible and always emotionally hard work.

People with autism can find it difficult to sustain a conversation or may swing around in the subtleties of the changing dynamic involved in such an interaction. They may appear awkward, gauche and unable to know what to do with themselves in a social setting. Other people with autism will not be concerned with what to do and, abandoning what others see as basic politeness, will proceed to interact regardless of status, appropriateness and the interests of the other party. Some people with autism may appear stilted, over-efficient or precise in their use of language and/or excessively formal in manner.

We are fundamentally social beings; while this may be becoming less so as we evolve, for the moment the inability to understand and read social interactions is a chronic and significant impairment affecting all areas of everyday functioning. Being ostracised by others, passed over for promotion, excluded from events or made to feel unwelcome directly because of this *impairment* could be considered discrimination.

Problems in thinking about and explaining their own behaviours

A sense of self enables us to be able to think about our own behaviours, thoughts and feelings and, to varying degrees, enables us to communicate or explain these to other people. When Jack cannot find his truck he can think about what he did with it last, recall memories of where he was playing with it and picture himself putting the truck away in the toy box. Jack can ask questions of himself having looked in his toy box and not found the truck: 'What was I doing, where was I playing, where did I put the truck?'

Sensing our own reactions and reading or thinking about our experiences enables us to regulate and consider our responses to other people and situations and learn from experiences that we are involved in.

To varying degrees, people with autism find it difficult to consider their own role in a situation; they have failed to develop what Jordan and Powell (1995) describe as an 'experiencing self'. They find it difficult not only taking in experiences but also asking questions of themselves about those experiences. In this way many people with autism have problems transferring something they have learnt in one situation to another; they cannot always rely on previous experiences to make judgements about what they should do in new situations.

Being able to give an account of ourselves is a useful attribute in all walks of life; having impairments in this area and without adaptations being in place can lead to significant disabilities.

Inability to gauge levels of interest

People with autism find it difficult to measure the levels of interest, usually in a verbal communication, that another person might have in what they are saying. Because they are interested in the subject it is easy to assume that someone else is also interested and to the same degree.

The ability to judge if someone else is sharing the same level of interest, attention or curiosity about what you are saying is an important way to form all sorts of relationships. Not being able to make those judgements (or make the subject interesting) – especially among children – can lead to being ostracised by one's peers. Wearing other people down with a wall of information on a topic that other people have no interest in can lead to additional social problems. For some people with autism, knowing that other people do not have an interest in the subjects that they like to talk about at length and in detail can compound their social isolation.

Taking into account what other people might know

If Jack's mother had seen that Oscar had left the truck in the garden she might well have told Jack the whereabouts of his truck. She can take into account that what is on *her* mind, is *not* on Jack's. What she knows, Jack doesn't. And so she will *share* information about the truck with Jack.

Some people with autism will not be able to consider that what *they* have seen or experienced and what is on *their* minds is not necessarily on someone else's. They may see no need or reason to share or give the information. Also people with autism may be unable to judge how much another person *does* know about a subject and are vulnerable to presenting themselves as being excessively patronising, arrogant and belittling.

This has obvious implications for everyday life: intelligent children with autism can come across in class as quite dim, while a fellow employee might consider the person with autism as secretive, uncooperative or plain rude.

Sharing attention

Jack's mother emerges from the changing rooms in a clothes shop wearing a dress she is trying on and wants to buy for a family event. She says to Jack's father, her husband: 'What do you think?' He says: 'I think we should buy Oscar a toy box.'

Bear with me. Here there has been a failure in shared attention. Jack's father has made an odd comment because he has failed to pick up on the object to which his wife is attending. (We might say he is distracted.)

People with autism may do this a lot of the time. They fail to join in and attend to the same thing to which everyone else is focused on. They find it difficult to pick up the gist of what is going on and so when they are asked for an opinion on the engineering drawings for a new car – and while everyone is thinking about the overall look – the person with autism may comment on the quality of the drawn lines and miss the point to which everyone else is attending.

In schools and colleges a common problem for learners with autism is knowing when the teacher is referring to them 'as well'. For example a learner with autism may start talking at the same time as the teacher because he doesn't realise that the teacher is talking to the whole class.

Anticipating other people's opinions of one's behaviours and reading emotions

A man called Martin paced in an unusually eccentric and rapid manner in a busy high street as he waited for his bus. When he started catching this bus he had become depressed and concerned that people were giving him 'funny looks'. He became increasingly persecuted by these looks; so much so that he began to miss the bus he had to catch for work.

Martin could not work out for himself that his 'style' of pacing was the source of other people's reactions to him.

In the example given earlier involving Oscar, Jack and a toy truck, Oscar does not anticipate that his brother Jack might be upset if he leaves the truck outside in the garden. Oscar may have not yet developed an understanding that what he does forms other people's opinions of him. (Though clearly leaving your brother's best truck out in the garden gives us some indication that Oscar will develop this ability quickly.)

In people with autism, a theory of mind has not developed. They can fail to take into consideration what other people know and think. Because of this some people with autism, to varying degrees, can fail to understand that their own behaviours affect other people, often significantly. They may appear to lack a conscience, come across as callous and may not be motivated to please another person.

> A young man with autism was looking forward to meeting his new social worker. His teacher, his mother, a learning support tutor and the school careers officer were present. When his social worker walked in the door she was immediately and excitedly greeted as the young man rushed to shake her hand with 'Wow, aren't you fat!'

It took the considerable social skills of his teacher to persuade the social worker that, while it seemed that way, this was not a deliberate act of insolence and that the young man in question was unable to work out that what he said was hurtful. He thought he was just stating the obvious. Cumine *et al.* (1998) in their excellent guide *Asperger Syndrome: A Practical Guide for Teachers* cite the example of a boy they call Michael who used to trip his brother down the stairs unaware that it would hurt – he simply wanted to know how many times his brother banged his head. Misunderstanding or being unable to read or feel the emotional impact of other people is a severe impairment.

Reading other people's intentions and motives

Being able to read the intentions of other people helps us in all kinds of situations. It prevents us from being conned, hoodwinked and deceived and in turn enables us to understand and influence other people. Knowing what people are going to do is one thing; knowing why is altogether more complicated.

Some people with autism find the subtle nature of friendship, deceit, jokes, humour, white lies or even blatant bullying and harassment difficult to understand. As a result of not being able to read clearly what the intentions of other people might be, many people with autism can find themselves getting into trouble with the law, having problems at school or missing out on the nuances of office politics.

> A schoolboy set fire to a school waste bin because his 'friends' told him it would be fun. He doesn't realise that he has been set up by the others and he is unaware not only that he has been duped but also that he will be in trouble with the school.

Differentiating fact from fiction

At some point as children around 3 years old, we learn to distinguish between real things we can touch and things that we can think about but cannot touch. For some people with autism being able to grasp the idea of things being real and false is difficult. People with autism have problems representing. The idea of 'acting' may be a difficult concept for some children with autism to grasp, and distinguishing between when someone is pretending or not is a problem.

Having difficulties relating internal states of mind to external states of affairs may also mean that a person with autism may struggle to see that what they think is not true.

Patricia Howlin *et al.* (1999) cite the example of Michael – presumably not the same as cited by Cumine *et al.* (1998) – who has problems understanding misunderstandings.

> Michael lost his job after attacking a cloakroom attendant who had given him the wrong ticket. He showed no remorse or comprehension that a 'mistake' had been made. Michael could not read the 'reality' of the situation as seen by everyone else; he could not share the misunderstanding.

Predicting people's behaviours

In our example at the beginning of the chapter, Jack might be able to imagine and forecast what his brother Oscar has done based on previous experience. When Jack finds that his truck is not in the toy box where he left it, he may deduce that Oscar has had it and left it somewhere. A child with autism would find Jack's mental feat of speculation difficult. Knowing what other people are going to do involves being able to read their intentions, their beliefs and the situation they are in and so make inferences about people's future actions.

We can predict that when Jack comes home from school he will look for his truck. We can do this because we know he believes that that is where it is because that is where he left it. We have a theory about his mind, we can think about his thoughts and beliefs and predict intentions. Many people with autism will find this task difficult.

Being unable to predict or make sense of what other people will do can result in many people with autism being in a constant state of anxiety and, often, surprise. People with autism may avoid others, because they might be frightened of them, and often prefer activities that do not involve other people or certainly exhibit people-avoiding behaviours.

Summary

The theory of mind gives us a good idea of the problems people with autism come up against in everyday life. For people with autism who may not be able to read the intentions of others or make sense easily of relationships and social situations, how will they know they might be being discriminated against?

Central coherence

Put simply *central coherence* is the psychological process by which we make meaning and we are able to see the whole picture (Frith 1989). It is the process by which we take in various types of information, say for example in a story, and pull the information together to get the *gist*, the general idea, instead of recalling every single detail or just the odd fragment.

Leo Kanner (1943), who was the first to give a complete description of autism, highlighted one of the core features of autism to be the 'inability to experience wholes without full attention to the constituent parts' (Happé 1994, p.127).

As Lorna Wing (1981) has observed, in autism there is a failure to 'Seek out experiences and make a coherent story' (Wing 1981, quoted in Happé 1994, p.127). It is said that people with autism have weak cohesive abilities: 'The normal operation of central coherence compels us human beings to give priority to understanding meaning. Hence we can easily single out meaningful from meaningless material' (Frith 1989, p.101).

It should be noted that the ability to focus on just detail has some considerable advantages, and in people with autism can lead to quite amazing 'islets of abilities' (Happé 1994, p.43). However, the ability to draw diverse pieces of information together and make them meaningful or to take different pieces of information and paint a complete picture is a feat many people with autism find very difficult.

The following sections discuss the implications of having a weak central coherence.

Problems linking information and seeing connections

Skills can become context specific and people with autism may not see that a skill learnt in one situation could be relevant and useful in another. In educational circles this is often referred to as difficulties in 'generalising' or 'transferring' knowledge. This can extend to many situations; although a person with autism may have mastered the task in one setting, it does not automatically follow that the same task can be performed in a different setting or context.

Problems organising self, experiences, materials and tasks

Without being able to see the bigger picture, it is difficult to know how to gather together the things that will be needed in carrying out some simple tasks. Getting ready to go to work in the morning requires multi-tasking. Being at work could then involve holding a task in mind, pulling together the ingredients needed to complete that task, executing the task, discussing it with others, seeing their point of view, debating different views, worrying about other people's motives and wondering how to make an impression.

People with autism find this difficult and can often appear to procrastinate. They may have difficulties getting started, get lost or confused easily, get stuck on one particular detailed task to the detriment of the overall task being achieved and become quite anxious that the task is not getting done.

Strong preference for the known and avoidance of novelty

Kanner has said that as a result of their fragmentary processing, once a procedure has become established there follows a resistance to allow for change: 'a situation, a performance…is not regarded as complete if it is not made up of exactly the same elements that here present at the same time…[they were] first confronted with it' (Happé 1994, p.127).

Many people with autism feel the need to stick to the same routines or procedures once they have become established. In a world that appears fragmented and often meaningless, it is not surprising that habit and routine become essential prerequisites to everyday functioning.

The need for sameness can also extend to many areas of life; people with autism may like to wear the same clothes over and over and/or always eat the same foods. Again in a fragmentary world where one's own experiences may be as equally confusing, many people with autism have come to rely on and be comforted by the familiarity of the known. In this way doing new things, undertaking new tasks or trying something different can become insurmountable.

It should be noted that the problems that people with autism have in these areas are not just a question of dented or hurt feelings. The anxiety and fear generated by a change in routine or the imposition of some novelty can cause real constitutional trauma.

Trouble in prioritising or choosing

Without holding in mind the general idea behind something, it is difficult to know what elements of that idea will be more important than others and so making a choice between constituent parts becomes difficult. This might also extend to having an overall idea about oneself. People with poor central coherence have experiences that feel fragmented and confusing. Making a decision about something or choosing between things can become an impenetrable feeling of bewilderment and an insurmountable task.

Some people with autism have come to rely on complex systems, habits or cataloguing procedures in order to overcome this problem of choice and feelings of fragmentation. Unfortunately some of these systems and habits often might not fit in the context in which they are being used.

Narrow focus of attention

In the workplace an employee may not seem to be able to pull in the same direction as other employees (obviously this can also make for a very creative individual). Employees with autism often need quite clear guidelines of precisely what their job involves and exactly what is the nature of the task they are required to perform. In the middle of a heated debate about 'Policy and Recrutment', the person with autism is the person who, in the middle of it all, points out that the word recruitment is wrongly spelt.

Many teachers report that the child with autism in their class will not always be able to focus on the same thing as the other children; the child with autism will not always get the point of a task in the same way that the other children may pick it up. Many people with autism have very narrow fields of interests that border on obsessions and do not chime with the interests of other people easily; these obsessions may often be presented at times that seem highly inappropriate.

Lack of compliance

People with autism may not be able to picture themselves in a situation and see how it is that they might 'come across' to others. We all have some sense of what other people think of us and gauge our responses and actions accordingly. Many people with autism do not. They do not always comply with the expected ways of behaving since they fail to see the bigger picture.

You only have to read about the trouble that people with autism get into in different situations in the various websites on the subject to appreciate the problems and difficulties people with autism have in complying with what is expected.

The person with autism will not always be able to conform to the implicit unwritten but expected rules of behaviour in a given context. This can be as embarrassing for the person with autism as it may be for others and can obviously lead to serious problems.

Point of view

We all see things from our own point of view though we do not always impose our perspective on something or always bring a topic of conversation around to what we want to talk about. People with autism do. If we are capable of seeing things from another person's point of view, we are equally capable of adjusting (or interfacing) our point of view with another's. People with autism find this difficult.

Not appreciating that someone else does not think the same things as you can lead to a number of problems. In a world that appears to be fragmented and whose meaning may be difficult to grasp, it is difficult for many people with autism to form coherent points of view and more difficult to communicate this. As one student finally managed to say after many frustrating hours: 'I can't do it and I can't tell you how I can't do it.'

The insistence of imposing their own routine habits and ways of doing things on any given situation or relationship can be very difficult for people to live with and without the right interventions, family life with an adolescent with autism can test parenting skills to the limit.

Summary

In the 'theory of mind' we saw how autism impairs the ability to relate to other people in the usual expected ways. With 'central coherence' we see some of the more practical problems that are faced by people with autism in functioning in everyday life.

> I once gave an envelope that needed posting to a student and asked him: 'Could you post this for me on your way to lunch?', knowing that the student knew where the post box was – a few roads away and on the way to the sandwich shop. After looking at the envelope the student said simply: 'Yes.' He did not return after lunch! The police were called and a search party set off. Eventually he turned up – having posted the letter to the actual address on the envelope – some three miles away.

Executive functioning

Executive functioning is the mental ability we all have to plan actions, organise and respond, monitor and control ourselves, be flexible in our thinking, research and deal with change. Problems with poor executive functioning (as with central coherence) occur within the normal population and among people with other impairments, especially people with learning disabilities. However, coupled with problems of communication, the theory of mind and central coherence, for people with autism, problems related to poor executive functioning are chronic.

People with autism tend to be 'perseverative' where problems are concerned. That is, they tend to repeat strategies to problems that have already failed. Harris (1993) cites a study by Russell *et al.* (1991) which illustrates the problem well. A child is asked to choose between two boxes that the child can see into. One box is empty, the other has a sweet in it. To succeed in gaining the sweet as a prize, the child is asked to choose the box that is *empty*. Most of the children with autism failed time and time again, and continued to choose the box with the sweet in it, even though they knew this meant they failed. What is happening here is that children with autism cannot suspend their desire and reconfigure their thoughts to *hold in mind* the idea that by *not* choosing the sweet, they win the sweet.

Difficulties in holding on to or imagining future events

Significantly people with impairments in executive functioning are said to 'have difficulty in guiding their current behaviour in terms of…a non-existent but foreseeable context' (Harris 1993, p.235). In other words, they have difficulty holding something in mind and thinking about it in the future and then in deciding what to do about it.

Not being able to hold a set of actions in mind (think about) or hold a series of events in the short-term memory can lead to problems of imitation. Copying or imitating involves holding in mind the behaviour seen and then reproducing it through coordinating one's own actions. Some people with autism will find this difficult.

Similar to theory of mind, with poor executive functioning the ability to perceive emotions is also impaired. In order to understand what someone else is feeling, you need to be able to read the pattern of their expressions and then match them to those held in mind or their own mental states. People with autism find this very difficult (Jordan and Powell 1995, p.94).

Pretending or simulating can be meaningless

In order to pretend at something, you need to be able to imagine the 'real' situation being played out. This is a complex executive function. Pretending to do something or simulating a real situation involves thinking about a real object or a situation, holding onto the thought and then representing it in a new 'false' situation.

Pretending and simulating can be totally meaningless to some people with autism. Teaching people with autism out of the context in which the skills that are being taught are needed can be pointless. The implications for education and training are obviously significant.

Planning, starting, stopping and moving from one task to another

Problems with executive functioning can lead to problems of planning and organising. These tasks involve holding a series of future events in mind and then executing them. Simple everyday tasks such as getting your things ready to go out to work or to school can become very difficult for people with autism. (Note here that the abilities of people with autism of establishing routines, patterns of behaviours and habits can be enormously beneficial in this respect.) Unless it is particularly and literally obvious moving on to another task involves a whole new set of mental schema. Switching from what you are doing to another task again involves holding things in mind and imagining or putting yourself in a position of doing something else. This is hard work for people with autism.

Stopping or knowing when the job is done, especially where the task is unclear (such as in a conversation), can be especially difficult for people with autism. In this way people with autism can often be described as being inflexible in their thinking. They get stuck thinking the same ways and find it difficult to change their minds.

Problems of impulsivity

Without being able to plan a series of steps to achieve something or take what we might see as an appropriate 'course of action', people with autism can appear to act extremely impulsively. Often people with autism may not be able to regulate their responses to all manner of stimuli, for example touching other people at the most inappropriate moment.

Summary

In the 'theory of mind' we saw how autism impairs the ability to relate to other people in the usual expected ways. With 'executive functioning' we see some of the more practical problems that are faced by people with autism in everyday functioning and how they can be pervasive.

Conclusions

Autism is a profound impairment of a person's ability to relate in the usual ways to other people and the world. It is useful to return to Lorna Wing's triad to summarise autism. There are impairments in:

- getting along socially with other people

- general communication

- using the imaginative capacities to organise, plan and regulate oneself.

It is well known that people with autism can be unusually sensitive to light, sound, touch and other sensory issues, which can play a major part in their abilities to function effectively. These are loosely called additional sensory impairments. Many people with autism and Autistic Spectrum Disorders have problems integrating sensory information. Sensory problems can bring about considerable levels of stress and the need to reduce these levels of stress by making adjustments to the levels of stimulation they experience may be considered a reasonable adjustment (see Chapter 2). But also with many sensory integration problems there are many common-sense everyday solutions.

> A man with autism, Karl, was unable to attend a college course because he couldn't get there due to the crowds and the noise. Social services wouldn't pay for transport because his IQ was too high and his local college did not offer the course in engineering he wanted to do. His father eventually persuaded the rest of the family that Karl should do his CBT (Compulsory Basic Training for motorcyclists). Karl did it, passed it, Dad bought him a cheap moped and so Karl got into college every day.
>
> Another man with autism was given driving lessons as a part of his specialist college course. This student was not going to be able to work in any busy environments nor use public transport. He eventually did pass his driving test and now makes a living as a van driver, courier and delivery man.
>
> Another student who disliked touching was taught to say: 'I do not like being touched and I do not shake hands.' Once most people knew this, it didn't happen.

2

The Law

Nicholas Graham

Introduction

This chapter has two purposes. The first is to provide step-by-step answers to the question: what is disability discrimination? You may not have articulated the question in that way before, but if you have ever tried to resolve, for example, an employment dispute – as an employee with disabilities, or as an employer of a person with disabilities – and you have sat back, scratched your head and wondered whether the world has gone mad, then deep down you probably need to know the answer to the question: what is discrimination?

If you are a person with a disability the answer to that question is more easily felt than it is explained: you feel uncomfortable with the way you are treated at work, or (if you are a parent) the way your child with a disability is treated at school, but you are told that everyone has been treated the same way and so it is fair and you have no business to complain. Or, perhaps, you are an employer or a head teacher and you have been told you cannot do something (which seems eminently sensible and in the interests of other employees or pupils) because it would fall foul of the disability legislation.

If you are facing those or similar circumstances, then this chapter is aimed at restoring your sanity by giving you an outline of the concepts and principles that determine what amounts to discrimination – so you can avoid it if you are responsible for providing services, employment or education to people with disabilities or so you can complain about it if you have suffered from it as someone with a disability. Inevitably this chapter has much legal jargon and may be heavy going if you are not used to reading legal terminology.

The second purpose of this chapter is to illustrate the particular problems that people with autism face. Much of the disability discrimination legislation and case law has focused on people with a physical disability or, to use the wording in the Disability Discrimination Act 1995, 'physical impairment'. We looked at the difference between disability and social impairment in Chapter 1.

However, much of modern life – be it in work, education or even, say, accessing transport – requires an understanding of complex social interactions. For those with autism it is their impairments that immediately place them at a disadvantage in those social situations. Set out below is an attempt at how the law addresses that issue.

The disability discrimination legislation

On 30 March 2007 the UK government signed the UN Convention on the Rights of Persons with Disabilities, which sets out 'to promote, protect and ensure the full and equal enjoyment of all human rights and fundamental freedoms by all persons with disabilities, and to promote respect for their inherent dignity'.

The UN Convention is supposed to provide enforceable rights, but the impact of signing up to the Convention is likely to be minimal as since the mid-1990s the UK has sought to protect the rights of disabled people by the Disability Discrimination Act 1995 (DDA). Although there was some legislation and case law in the employment field prior to 1995 that provided some protections, these were rarely observed.

The provisions of the DDA were not all enacted at once and the rights enshrined in the original 1995 Act have been built on since. Following various amendments disabled people are now afforded protection in the areas of

- employment

- education

- access to goods, facilities and services including transport services

- buying and renting land or property.

The new Disability Discrimination Act 2005 also ensures that all aspects of the public sector activities take into account the needs of people with disabilities along with the positive duty (as with the UN Convention) to promote equality of opportunity for those people.

The principles

As with all legislation, the task for courts and tribunals is to interpret that legislation and apply it to the many and various disputes that they deal with every day. And it would be fair to say that those working with the DDA have struggled to understand the more complicated aspects of it.

The Act was the first piece of equalities legislation since the Race Relations and Sex Discrimination Acts introduced in the mid-1970s. In part, the Act makes similar provisions – the general prohibition against discrimination on the grounds of disability, that is, less favourable treatment on the grounds of disability. But there are radically new provisions: the concept of *reasonable adjustments* is a novel concept in discrimination law.

As indicated above, the DDA covers many areas and the principles below are common to all the areas – employment, education, service provision. However, there are some unique features of the legislation that apply to each individual area which this chapter cannot address in detail. An excellent starting point to look at additional rights and duties in any given area is the Equality and Human Rights Commission website or the DirectGov website.

What is a disability? Is autism a disability?

It is only those people with a disability who are able to rely on the protection afforded by the DDA. Whether you have a disability, therefore, is critical as to what rights you may rely on or what obligations you may have under the Act.

As we saw in Chapter 1, Section 1 of the DDA defines a 'disabled person' as:

> (1) Subject to the provisions of Schedule 1, a person has a disability for the purposes of this Act if he has a physical or mental impairment which

UNIVERSITY OF WINCHESTER
LIBRARY

has a substantial and long-term adverse effect on his ability to carry out normal day-to-day activities.

(2) In this Act 'disabled person' means a person who has a disability. (Disability Discrimination Act 1995 (c.50). Part one, section one)

Schedule 1 analyses the component elements of that definition.

In terms of impairment, normally reference is made to various bodies that have lists of what might amount to a 'condition' for the purposes of the DDA. There is even a set of regulations about what is excluded from the definition of a disability. For our purposes, the point to note is that autism *is not* excluded as a condition covered by Section 1 and Schedule 1.

What is a *substantial adverse effect*? This will, in most cases, be a matter of fact for the court or tribunal to determine.

What is *long term*? Long term is defined as 12 months or more, or where the disability is likely to last for the life of the disabled person if this is less than 12 months. As autism is a lifelong condition, this provision would be satisfied.

What are *normal day-to-day activities*? To meet this criteria the impairment must significantly impact on a number of areas – for mental impairments the most important activities are those requiring an ability to concentrate, learn or understand or to have a perception of risk or danger. As we have seen in Chapter 1, having autism has a significant impact on day-to-day functioning.

People with autism vary in their abilities – they are on a spectrum – so it would be possible to envisage circumstances where someone with high-functioning autism may have a mental impairment but it does not have a substantial impact on their day-to-day activities.

Under powers granted by the DDA, statutory Guidance and a Code of Practice have been issued. The Guidance urges courts and tribunals to look closely at the question of whether a disability is *substantial*, whether it is long term and what is the effect on normal day-to-day activities.

The Guidance points out that to determine whether a disability has a substantial adverse effect on a person's abilities would involve an analysis of both the time taken to carry out an activity and consideration of the way that activity is carried out.

Section 1, Schedule 1, the Code of Practice and the Secretary of State's Guidance all would lend support to an argument that those with an

Autistic Spectrum Disorder would ordinarily fall within the provisions of the Act.

To put matters beyond doubt, the case of Hewett v. Motorola Ltd (2004) which was heard in the Employment Appeal Tribunal confirmed that difficulties in understanding were not limited to difficulties in understanding information or knowledge, but included difficulties in understanding social interactions. We explore this case in detail below.

What is discrimination?

In the disability arena discrimination is the unlawful treatment of another person. That unlawful treatment is manifest in two ways.

- The first is known as *less favourable* treatment, which is treating a person with a disability less favourably as compared to someone without a disability.

- The second is apparent when there is a failure in the obligation to make a *reasonable adjustment*.

It is the case, unfortunately, that many people are treated badly or unreasonably and because someone is simply a bad employer or unfriendly shop assistant, such treatment may not necessarily amount to discrimination.

> *Where it can be shown that the treatment afforded to someone is due to their disability, then people with disabilities can seek the protection of the legislation.*

Reasonable adjustment is unlike other equalities legislation and this duty is imposed where some adjustment to, say, the working environment, can be made which ensures that the person with the disability is not placed at a substantial disadvantage as compared to someone without a disability.

It is worth mentioning two other forms of discrimination. The first is known as *victimisation* and it refers to circumstances where you suffer some form of detriment at work because you have supported someone who has made a complaint about the treatment given to them – maybe you have been a witness at a tribunal supporting a colleague who is alleging discrimination, for example.

The second form of discrimination is *harassment*. This is where the complaint is of unwelcome conduct by the accused which makes the disabled person uncomfortable or infringes their dignity in any way. Examples could be 'forcing' students to join in classes without allowing them time to acclimatise, or expecting people with autism to be sociable and then ostracising them when they are not. You can probably think of many more. Needless to say, both these forms of discrimination are unlawful.

What is less favourable treatment?

But what if I am a sensitive soul and am easily offended by what I perceive to be someone's aggressive management or 'loud' teaching style, a style that my more robust colleagues see as a 'can-do' attitude which is just what is needed? And who is to decide whether the treatment I get is less favourable?

The factual circumstances that might arise in any given situation are infinite so the legislation gives no list or category of the sort of actions or conduct that could amount to less favourable treatment. It can be related to any conduct which causes any justified sense of grievance. It includes things like not being selected for an interview, or not being allowed to attend a particular school, or being shunned or made fun of, or being overlooked for promotion. It can even include the way work is handed out to you by your manager, or having tasks taken off you or not being served in a restaurant or pub, or not being allowed into a building.

How you feel about the treatment will not necessarily determine whether your grievance was justified as that will ultimately be for a court or tribunal to decide. It is an objective rather than a subjective test, although whether the disabled person considers the treatment was less favourable will be an important factor to be taken into account. Each case is looked at on its own merits, taking into account all the facts of the case.

Under the DDA if you can establish less favourable treatment, then you can go to the next stage, which is to show that the less favourable treatment was *on the grounds* of your disability.

What does 'on the grounds of' mean?

It is perhaps the way of human nature, but the admission of unfavourable treatment is rarely forthcoming by the perpetrator of that treatment. It is almost unheard of for an employer to admit that the reason for the unfavourable treatment was related to a person's disability. (In the race discrimination field, there was an infamous case of an employer who advertised for a job but in the advertisement he excluded applicants who resided in a certain postcode from applying. Upon examination it transpired that the area covered by that particular postcode had a high percentage of people from ethnic minorities. While appearing to put forward a geographical reason for the unfavourable treatment, which was lawful, the real reason was on the grounds of race, which was not.)

So what is an employee with disabilities to do? How can he or she prove that the reason for not being selected for a post was discriminatory while the interview panel say that they thought the other candidate was 'better qualified' or 'demonstrated an understanding of the needs of the company'.

As indicated above, it is unlikely that an employer would admit that the treatment afforded was due to some disability. The employer is more likely to put forward some other reason. So, what is a tribunal or court to do? Most courts and tribunals are alive to the problem and they now require the person complaining about discrimination to make out their case – to outline why they consider their treatment was less favourable as compared to someone without a disability. If you identify the legitimate grievance or the specific conduct and have evidence about that, then the tribunal or court will turn to the other party – the accused, if you will – and ask for their reasons for the treatment.

The employer, school or service provider must then give their reasons for the treatment and the tribunal/court's task is to analyse that in detail to see if it is a credible, non-discriminatory reason for the treatment.

As indicated above, there is no list of legitimate reasons for not employing someone, or not admitting someone to a school. The judge must take into account all the surrounding circumstances of a case to determine whether discrimination has taken place. That involves a detailed examination of all the evidence and all the reasons provided, to see if they stack up.

If they don't, if the employer cannot provide a credible basis for their decision making, if all the accused can say is: 'Well, we thought he wouldn't be the right fit in the team, but it wasn't because we have anything against someone with a disability,' then a judge is not likely to find such an excuse satisfactory or credible and is now obliged to find that the real reason for the treatment is the person's disability.

An example

Take the case of Mark Isles (reported in *Ealing Times* 2006). Mark was a officer of the London Borough of Ealing who was not shortlisted for a vacancy he had applied for in the council (less favourable treatment) because of his Asperger syndrome (on the grounds of his disability), notwithstanding that he had done precisely the same job previously (without justification). The council's defence was a little confused; they first argued that Mr Isles' autism (in the form of Asperger syndrome) was too mild to be covered by the DDA (no substantial adverse effect) although they admitted that his Autistic Spectrum Disorder was the reason he was not considered suitable for the position.

The Tribunal ruled that Mr Isles' disability was substantial and he was therefore covered by the DDA. London Borough of Ealing failed to assess that disability and simply assumed what his capabilities were. Mark Isles was awarded £9000 compensation.

Who is a comparator?

Less favourable treatment on the grounds of disability is only the first limb of the test. Ironically, for claims of sex or race discrimination and other areas of discrimination law, it is a defence for an employer to respond to a claim of less favourable treatment by arguing that it treats all staff badly, regardless of race or sex. If the claimant cannot demonstrate that the less favourable treatment is for an unlawful reason, and is no different as compared to others, then they have no claim.

The obligation on the person claiming discrimination is to point to another person (in the case of a person with disabilities, a non-disabled person) and use them as a comparator. In effect, the comparator is someone to point to and say: 'You selected them for the interview and they are in the same position as me.'

The comparator can be real or hypothetical but must be someone in a similar situation. So, if an employee cannot perform as well, because of their disability, then any treatment they receive must be compared to someone who performs well or appropriately, because the reason for the poor performance is disability related.

In the case studies in Chapter 3 you will see how Antonio was being discriminated against when compared to other students with different disabilities since he was not given time to acclimatise to the college environment and people during his induction where other students had been given ramps, signers and so on. The same is also the case for Jonathon in Chapter 3.

What is disability-related discrimination?

Disability-related discrimination is the shorthand way of saying what is set out above. It is a term used in the DDA but it simply means less favourable treatment of a person for a reason related to their disability compared to a person without a disability.

Disability-related discrimination is normally self-evident. It can include the grosser types of treatment – the sort of treatment that would provoke a cry from any reasonable observer of, 'That is not fair.' Most workplaces or schools and service providers are alive to ill-treatment of disabled people. However, it still goes on. The former Disability Rights Commission website records a case of a child who had a disability being made to wear a red star band so that he could be identified in the playground. The boy's parents complained that the use of the band simply highlighted to others his disability and he found it humiliating. Needless to say the Tribunal criticised the school for that type of practice. There was no basis for it and it was clearly treatment that was less favourable. Other children who did not have the disability were not singled out by having to wear something that would identify them. A finding of disability-related discrimination was made against the school.

Disability-related discrimination can in certain circumstances (although not in the last example) be justified.

What amounts to a justification?

Justifying less favourable treatment is again something unique in discrimination legislation, unlike race or sex discrimination, where less favourable treatment can never be justified. However, in certain circumstances there may be genuine occupational reasons. Personal care of elderly people would be one example, where seeking a woman to provide care for an elderly woman would be permitted. If the accused can say that there was good reason (the DDA says that the reason for the treatment must be material or substantial) then the discriminatory treatment is not unlawful.

For physical disabilities, there are obvious examples. If the person with a disability cannot undertake an essential part of a job (for example, where a person's visual impairment precludes them from driving and the job requires the employee to drive) then not to recruit them for the post would be less favourable treatment on the grounds of disability as compared to someone who did not have that disability. However, the law does not say that that form of discrimination is unlawful. Such treatment *would* be justified.

For those with autism the problems are more subtle. Many jobs require good team working or good interpersonal skills as standard, essential or desirable competencies. If my disability is such that I am unable to demonstrate those skills, or I am seen as a poor performer and so overlooked for a promotion because of my poor social skills, then the essential question is whether that treatment is justified.

There is no easy answer. Some jobs may require considerable social competency, others may not. Some people with autism may have greater or lesser aptitude for social circumstances. It is all a matter of fact and degree.

What is a reasonable adjustment?

Before concluding whether the treatment is justified, the question of *reasonable adjustments* must be considered. Again, unknown in the area of equal opportunities, the DDA imposes an obligation on employers, schools and service providers to make *reasonable adjustments* so that the person with disabilities is not put at a substantial disadvantage, as compared to someone without a disability.

If the arrangements for admissions to schools or the policy or practice of an employer or service provider means that the person with disabilities is placed at a substantial disadvantage, then reasonable steps must be taken to address that disadvantage.

When first brought into force the failure to make reasonable adjustments could be justified. That has now been dropped as it was thought that the term 'reasonable' was sufficient to determine how far changes had to be made. However, it is not possible to prescribe what amounts to a reasonable adjustment in every potential situation that could arise. Codes of practice which tribunals and court must have regard to have been developed by the then Disability Rights Commission (now known as the Equality and Human Rights Commission). These give an ideal of the sorts of adjustments that could be made. This could include reallocating duties, redeployment, changing working hours, providing special equipment, providing supervision or support, adjusting interviews – see Chapter 4. Many adjustments are not costly and could be introduced without too much problem.

Employers and educators do require some imaginative planning to get it right, but with a positive attitude, it is in many cases easily accomplished.

What is reasonable?

What if the disability calls for adaptations that would be very costly to a small employer? What if the building works that were needed to make the adaptations were terribly disruptive? Those are all points that will inform the determination as to what is reasonable. The resources available, the disruption and the certainty of whether the adjustments will have the desired result – that is, whether they will ensure that the person with a disability is not substantially disadvantaged – all go into the mix.

David Perkins is manager of National Autistic Society (NAS) Prospects, a specialist employment scheme for people with autism; he reported in *Personnel Today*: 'Disappointingly, though, there is still resistance to employing people with disabilities. Some employers find it difficult to make the reasonable adjustments that would enable people with disabilities to work' (Perkins 2007). This may be true, but it is simply unlawful. Not making reasonable adjustments, difficult or not, is unlawful.

Autism and disability

The application of the above principles as they apply to those with autism was addressed in the seminal case of Hewett v. Motorola Ltd (UKEAT/05/0526/03/ILB).

The facts

Timothy Hewett worked in the electronics industry as an engineer and was employed by Motorola from August 2000 to October 2002, when he resigned. He made a number of complaints to the Tribunal while he was employed alleging disability discrimination. He claimed that his employer had failed to provided adequate training, supervision and support, had failed to make reasonable adjustments to employment policies and procedures and had discriminated against him in the way that it had monitored his performance in his appraisal.

The employer's response to his claim was simply to state that they did not consider that he had a disability for the purposes of the DDA. By implication that meant that he could not argue he had been treated less favourably on the grounds of his disability and, if they were right, they had no obligation to make reasonable adjustments to any of their work practices.

On 27 October 2002 Mr Hewett resigned and presented a further claim to the Tribunal alleging less favourable treatment and failures to make reasonable adjustments. The employer maintained the same line of defence as the previous claim and the two cases were consolidated.

What is impressive about Mr Hewett is that he brought the case on his own – drafting the claim to the Tribunal, managing the process to the final hearing and then representing himself at trial. It was even more impressive as he was up against one of the most experienced employment Queen's Counsel (senior barrister) employed by the employers.

The expert evidence

At the Employment Tribunal Mr Hewett relied on two medical experts – a consultant psychiatrist and his own general practitioner (GP). The consultant was of the view that he had many of the characteristics of autism and that this 'probably conforms to a diagnosis of Asperger's Syndrome'. The consultant went on to say that these autistic traits made him difficult to manage and to fit within an organisation and that he might require special assistance.

Mr Hewett's GP had seen the consultant's report and agreed with it and confirmed that, among other things, Mr Hewett had difficulties with social relationships and difficulty with communication and found it hard to understand 'non-verbal signals and "coded messages", including facial expressions, aspects of human interaction which for the majority of us are instinctive'. All these matters contributed to Mr Hewett's stress, fatigue and mental pain.

When looking at the effect that his autism (in the form of Asperger syndrome) had on his normal day-to-day activities, the GP confirmed that he did have problems in communication and paying attention 'particularly if instructions involve human assumptions and coded messages'. And, while he wanted to fit in, 'he only thrives when emotional overtones and coded messages are kept to a minimum. He can easily feel like an outsider'. Again, the GP confirmed that the effect of these problems was substantial as he had become isolated as an individual and that the effects were long term and had lasted for more than 12 months.

The employer relied on the report of a consultant developmental neuropsychiatrist, who was of the view that Mr Hewett was at the mild end of the autistic spectrum, which could be categorised as 'high-functioning autism'. The employer's consultant also minimised the effects that Mr Hewett's autism had on his normal day-to-day activities, saying that the effects were mild and indicating that:

> Were Mr Hewett expected to socialise, take part in small talk, initiate and sustain conversations, answer questions in a reciprocal manner, be expected to form and maintain relationships at a level beyond the concrete tasks that sustain him, manage people, lead a team, he would very likely, be inept. People with autistic traits are socially inept to a varying degree. They have some primary social deficits; they are inflexible, unyielding and stubborn. However, were his duties to be solitary, not requiring social interaction at a subtle level, clearly outlined and communicated in concrete, non ambiguous terms, and were he allowed to use his initiative and inventiveness, he should not have much difficulty.

Mr Hewett's evidence

Coupled with the expert evidence, Mr Hewett filed his own statement setting out some of the problems he experienced personally as a result of his disability, listed as follows:

- the difficulty in making and keeping friends which deprived him of the normal levels of support

- exclusion from normal social interactions which meant that he had to use a lot of energy reminding himself of the needs of others which in turn contributed to his level of stress

- his social interactions were stressful requiring considerable effort on his part to overcome his normal tendency to isolate himself which also in turn reduced his ability to pay attention

- he often came across to others as rude, which added to the cycle of exclusion and rejection.

As a result of these problems Mr Hewett had required time off work and had received the assistance of counselling services. Rather tragically he stated: 'Most of my life is spent as a solitary existence.'

The Employment Tribunal's decision

Having heard all the evidence the Tribunal concluded that Mr Hewett's ability to concentrate and his memory were impaired but that the impairment was not substantial as he had managed to fulfil the complex tasks of his job over a number of years and could remember names and facts and also had adapted to change in his working environment.

Significantly, the Tribunal accepted Mr Hewett's evidence that he had problems in communication and in social interaction. However, they went on to say that the DDA definition of a disability, mentioned in Section 1 of the DDA but elaborated upon in Schedule 1, made no mention of communication problems or difficulties in social interaction. They were, 'therefore, not matters that could be taken into account'. Accordingly, Mr Hewett's claims for disability discrimination were dismissed.

The Employment Appeal Tribunal's decision

The argument before the Employment Appeal Tribunal (EAT) was centred on the issue, as they put it, of 'whether an inability to understand through "the subtleties of human interaction" can fall within the definition of disability'.

The EAT reviewed the various legislative provisions – Section 1, Schedule 1 and the Guidance issued by the Secretary of State under Section 3 of the DDA. (That Guidance is specifically issued for the benefit of courts and tribunals to assist them in determining questions of disability, such as, whether the impairment was substantial, whether it had a substantial adverse and long-term effect.) The EAT also reviewed the Code of Practice for the elimination of discrimination issued, again, by the Secretary of State under Section 53 of the DDA.

It is worth setting out in detail what the Guidance and Code of Practice says about problems faced by those with autism. Since the case has been heard, the Secretary of State's Guidance and the Code of Practice have been revised. At the time the case was heard, the Guidance stated clearly that:

> Account should be taken of the person's ability to remember, organise his or her thoughts, plan a course of action and carry it out, take in new knowledge, or understand spoken or written instructions. This includes considering whether the person learns to do things significantly more slowly than normal. (s53)

Various examples were then listed of what would amount to a substantial adverse effect, including inability to remember names, inability to adapt after a reasonable period to minor changes in work routine.

The Code of Practice relevant at the time stated in general that:

> In some cases a reasonable adjustment will not work without the cooperation of other employees. Employees may therefore have an important role in helping to ensure a reasonable adjustment is carried out in practice. (*ibid.*)

And specifically for autistic employees the Code of Practice indicated that:

> It is a reasonable adjustment for an employee to communicate in a particular way to an employee with autism (a disability which can make it difficult for someone to understand normal social interaction among people). As part of the reasonable adjustment it is the responsibility of that employer to seek the co-operation of other employees in communicating in that way. (*ibid.*)

The EAT also had regard to an earlier case involving disability discrimination, Goodwin v. The Patent Office (1999), which urged tribunals to take a purposive approach to interpreting the legislation, taking fully into account the Secretary of State's Guidance and the Code of Practice.

Having reviewed the legislation, the other sources and the Guidance, the EAT came to the view that the Tribunal's decision that Mr Hewett's ability to concentrate was not substantial was one that they were entitled to reach. However, on the question of Mr Hewett's 'understanding', the EAT rejected the employer's argument that reference to this in the DDA and the Code of Practice and Guidance was simply a reference to learning and educational problems and did not refer to understanding complex social interactions.

According to the EAT the Tribunal had misunderstood the concept of 'understanding'; the EAT stated:

> someone who has a difficulty in understanding normal social interaction among people, and/or the subtleties of human non factual communication can be regarded as having their understanding affected and that concept is not limited to an ability to understand information, knowledge or instructions.

What the EAT could not do was determine whether the effect of Mr Hewett's problems in understanding social interactions was 'substantial' and remitted that question back to the Tribunal for reconsideration.

Conclusions

The DDA sets out to protect people with disabilities, including those with autism. The concepts and principles in the legislation as applied by the courts and tribunal will continue to refine and develop what can be a difficult area, particularly when the disability is autism. As the law stands at the moment, those with autism which has a substantial adverse effect on their day-to-day activities will have the protection afforded by the DDA; employers, service providers and educationalists, among others, have duties to consider what reasonable adjustments can be made to alleviate any disadvantage that a disability can have. Some actions will be justified, many will not. It can be costly – financially or otherwise – to ignore the DDA's important provisions.

Further protections are set out in the Disability Discrimination Act 2005. Since 4 December 2006 public authorities (including schools) have been under a general duty to promote disability equality, which includes promoting equality of opportunity and participation, promoting positive attitudes towards disabled people and eliminating discrimination and harassment. Local authorities and schools are now obliged to review their functions and look at other agencies they do business with in the light of this new duty. As well as the general duty there is a specific duty to publish a Disability Equality Scheme – an audit, if you like, of all the functions with indications as to how the duty relates to those functions. And there will be further developments.

At present compensation can be awarded by tribunals in the employ-ment context and by the county court where the discrimination complained of relates to the provision of further or higher education or the provision of goods or services. The Equalities and Human Rights Com-mission is currently consulting on whether compensation should be awarded to pupils with disabilities who successfully claim discrimination in schools, a claim currently dealt with by the Special Educational Needs and Disability Tribunal (SENDIST).

Also for schools, the present arrangements for exclusions are somewhat convoluted. Parents of a pupil with disabilities subject to per-manent exclusion can appeal to an independent appeal panel and argue that the decision to exclude should be overturned on the grounds that the reason for the exclusion was a reason related to the pupil's disability and if not justified then discriminatory. If, however, the exclusion was for a fixed term then the parents must complain to the Special Educational Needs and Disability Tribunal to get their remedy. The proposal is for all exclusions and disputes regarding admissions to be dealt with by the Tribunal.

These changes are unlikely to be brought into being by the Equalities and Human Rights Commission, which was set up under the DDA and given powers of enforcement similar to the Commission for Racial Equality and the Equal Opportunities Commission. In October 2007 all these bodies were brought under the wing of the Commission for Equality and Human Rights following the Single Equality Act that will serve (it is

UNIVERSITY OF WINCHESTER
LIBRARY

hoped) to unify the equalities legislation in a way that disabled people and those who are involved with them can better understand.

Useful websites

- A full copy of the text of the UN Convention can be found at www.un.org/esa/socdev/enable/rights/convtexte.htm (accessed 25.11.07).

- The full text of the DDA can be obtained from www.opsi.gov.uk (accessed 25.11.07) – note: this is the original 1995 text of the Act. It has now been extensively amended and the original text is out of date.

- Hewett v. Motorola Ltd – a full copy of the Employment Appeal Tribunal's judgment can be obtained from www.employmentappeals.gov.uk (accessed 25.11.07).

- The Disability Rights Commission has been superseded by the Equality and Human Rights Commission: see www.equalityhumanrights.com (accessed 25.11.07).

- The new Equality and Human Rights Commission website www.equalityhumanrights.com (accessed 25.11.07) has an enormous amount of information relevant to disability discrimination, the rights of disabled people together with links to the relevant legislation, Guidance and Code of Practice.

- Codes of practice cover schools and colleges, employers and service providers and are available from www.equalityhumanrights.com (accessed 25.11.07).

- The article by David Perkins (2007) is available from www.personneltoday.com (accessed 25.11.07)

Case Studies

Introduction

If you make use of a wheelchair it is relatively easy to see how and why services could adapt and make adjustments to their physical surroundings to enable you to gain access. This is true for most people with a *physical* impairment.

Autism is not a physical impairment; it is largely *social*. It is therefore much harder for non-autistic people, services, schools, employers, local authorities, shops, cinemas and others to think about the 'how and why' of providing access through making social adaptations and avoiding treating people with autism less favourably and so discriminating against them. It is doubly hard for many people with autism to be able to think about how and why other people might make adaptations for them (recall the theory of mind difficulties).

One of the purposes of this chapter is to show how in some cases many of the behaviours of people with autism that may be seen by some as 'anti-social', 'silly', 'offensive' or 'naughty', arise as a result of adaptations and adjustments *not* being in place and from the person being treated less favourably in comparison with other people without autism.

If you think that your son or daughter has been labelled 'silly' or has been described as 'naughty' when in fact they are behaving in ways that arise as a result of their autism, you might now like to consider this discrimination.

This chapter illustrates how someone with impairments of theory of mind, central coherence and executive functioning can become disabled by certain adjustments *not* being in place, and given their responsibilities under the Disability Discrimination Act 1995, leaves the institution open to accusations of discrimination.

The following combined case studies will illustrate how many of the behaviours that were originally seen as worthy of some form of disciplinary proceedings arose as a result of the person's impairment, their hard-wired difficulties. (However, people with autism, like any other groups in the population, have their fair share of antisocial behaviours that do not arise from any impairment but may relate to personality, age, culture or lifestyle.)

This chapter will illustrate how *adjustments* were made for three people at different points on the autism spectrum who were struggling at a general further education college, in a workplace and in a day centre. These case studies illustrate the ways in which people with autism can often present their difficulties where they are being treated less favourably when compared with others – including other people with disabilities – and raise important issues in the planning of services. There are three case studies:

- Antonio, who has 'typical' autism and attends a further education college

- Jonathon, who has Asperger syndrome and works as an administrative assistant

- Susan, who has autism and additional severe learning disabilities and attends a day centre.

The format of each case study is:

- brief description

- presenting behaviours at college, work or the day centre

- how these behaviours relate to autism

- the reasonable adjustments made.

Reasonable adjustments are those arrangements that need to be put in place in order to avoid the accusation that someone is treating people with autism less favourably than others and is therefore being discriminatory. Previously one might have said that these *reasonable adjustments* were 'educational approaches', 'interventions' or 'methods of providing support'. These days they must be considered legal duties. It is fair to say that speculating on how the behaviours being exhibited by someone related to their autism (the impairments in theory of mind, central coherence and executive functioning) takes considerable experience. At the end of this chapter there is a discussion of the implications of these case studies for further education colleges, schools and employers.

Note

The material for the three case studies, simplified for the purposes of this book, arose from a series of consultations that I undertook and have been added to from a composite of people and anecdote from various people who have worked with them. *They bear no relationship to any one person specifically.*

Antonio

Brief description

Antonio was 17 years old and diagnosed as autistic. Before college he had been at a special school, which he had attended most of his childhood. The transition of Antonio from school to college appeared to have gone well. The college had a link-day with the school and pupils could attend in their last term one day a week to acclimatise to the college environment; Antonio always attended. It amounted to about six days in total. After completing the college's standard initial 'assessment of need', Antonio was enrolled on the college's regular basic skills course.

From reports and information submitted to the college from the school, Antonio had autism with mild to moderate learning disabilities. He had a good, functional level of literacy and numeracy. He was reliant on routine and on prompts from staff. He found it difficult to organise his work and on the whole did the same things at the same time with the same people. The report stated that he also found it difficult to concentrate on instructions, that is on what the teacher was saying when in classes and groups.

After four weeks into the first term directly after completing his college induction problems began to arise.

Presenting behaviours at college

ANTONIO BEGAN SLAMMING DOORS

This happened during the unstructured times such as lunch, after he had finished eating, and sometimes at break after he had finished his cup of tea. He would stand by the fire doors leading into the canteen and begin slamming them into the frame. Staff reported how it was difficult to stop him straight away and he got away with not being escorted out immediately by security because he was a 'special needs' student. Linked to this he often couldn't move on from break or lunchtime with the other students from his group and back into his lessons in time without finishing what he was doing or without considerable prompting and cajoling.

ANTONIO COULD BECOME DISRUPTIVE IN CLASS

He would suddenly start singing at the top of his voice: the songs were not easily recognisable. Sometimes he would hide under the table. He often displayed a repertoire of other behaviours unrelated to anything to do with the lesson, the task or whatever the teacher considered appropriate. It was difficult for the teacher to understand and make sense of these behaviours (Antonio could not explain why he was doing them) and when they occurred they were extremely disruptive for the other students.

ANTONIO SEEMED UNMOTIVATED BY MANY OF THE TASKS

He could not get started where the tasks the teacher set were new. He would sit and refuse to start the work and occasionally collapse his body onto the desk and seem to 'pretend' to fall asleep.

ANTONIO STARTED WANDERING OFF

Throughout the college he would wander into places that he was not allowed. He would wander off at break times, sometimes at lunchtime and often if the class was moving from one place to another or at the beginning of the day. He found the Accounts and Finance department and the staff rooms; he frequently wandered into the kitchen behind the canteen. The consequences were missing lessons, disruption to lessons and security being called.

COMMENT

It would be easy to assume that these behaviours were wilfully antisocial, disobedient and purposefully disruptive and, since he was an adolescent, this was possible. However, in this instance Antonio's behaviours seemed far too extreme for a person with an autistic impairment to be considering in such a large public further education college and at which he had only recently started. They certainly didn't seem like the behaviours of a non-disabled 'normally disruptive' adolescent of his own age either. After the fifth week Antonio was suspended pending a review.

How these behaviours relate to autism

While there are no hard and fast rules to making sense of these complex behaviours we can, based upon what we know about autism, speculate.

SLAMMING DOORS

There is clearly an impairment of communication! Slamming doors is not how one usually gets attention. If he was distressed, why didn't Antonio seek help from a member of staff? He may not have known what 'help' was? Did he realise that the help he got at home or had previously received at school he could get at the college? Antonio might have been able to see things only from his own point of view and technically he may not have been able to see how his actions were adversely affecting others (a theory of mind problem).

We saw how people with autism find transferring information and knowledge and skills from one situation to another and in this scenario Antonio might be expecting the college break times to be the same as he had experienced at his school. He may have been trying to impose his experiences on a situation rather than adapting to it (a problem of executive functioning). It was noted in his school report that he was often prompted what to do next, when to finish his tea and when to start something else. In effect the school managed the unstructured time for him. This indicated that Antonio did have impairments in his executive functioning and that he may not have been taught or shown how he could ask for help in this new situation at college.

We can say then that door slamming was a manifestation of Antonio's anxiety at not knowing what to do next in that situation and not knowing how to ask for help. (As we saw in Chapter 1: not being able to ask for help because of theory of mind and executive functioning difficulties is a real hard-wired impairment.)

We have seen in Chapter 1 how people with autism found moving from one task to another or switching from one subject to another was an impairment of executive functioning. Antonio does not automatically know how to move on from his break or lunch and on to another task and had not been provided with any prompts or reminders. He could not easily gather his thoughts, coordinate and marshal his actions and then point them in the expected direction of whatever was going to happen next.

The unwritten rules of an institution would not necessarily be understood by someone with autism (*lack of compliance*), and related to impairments of central coherence. Antonio did not pick up the various types of information and cues in the environment or from other people that would indicate to him that what he was doing was wrong.

What we do know is that people with autism find it difficult to coordinate themselves to new settings, people and tasks. Given that Antonio had just started at the college, it was worth asking if Antonio had yet acclimatised or got used to the college routine. Had his induction been sufficient?

DISRUPTIVE IN CLASS

As further questions were asked about what happened in class in more detail, it became apparent that Antonio did not know what to concentrate on in the lessons. Because of problems related to central coherence and executive functioning, Antonio didn't know the teacher was talking to him when she was talking to the whole class. Note: this was not highlighted as a problem at the school because he had learnt that when the teacher was talking to the class at school, she also meant him. College was not school. Antonio had not generalised this knowledge. And linking what happened at school to what happened in college had not been a part of the induction.

It was also thought that despite the differences between school and college, Antonio might still expect the lessons to be the same at college as they were in school – impairments in both executive functioning and central coherence.

We know that Antonio may have had problems knowing what to concentrate on from his school report. He may also simply have not known that the behaviours he was exhibiting were not 'appropriate' for the classroom, no matter how entertaining for him and some of the other students. Did Antonio know what his job as a student was? Did he understand the role of the college tutor?

There was also much use by the teacher at the college of abstract expressions: 'soon', 'can we think about', 'what would happen if'. This possibly made it hard for Antonio to work out what the teacher was talking about: an executive functioning problem.

UNMOTIVATED BY MANY OF THE TASKS

Many people with autism see things from their own point of view and develop what appear to be motivational problems. Antonio did not see how what he was being asked to do related to him nor how he would benefit from doing it. This is strongly linked to problems of executive functioning and dealing with the novelty of unfamiliar and new tasks. How did the task in the lessons relate to Antonio's interests? Did Antonio know how he was going to benefit?

Antonio's teachers felt that he just didn't see the point of doing the task. It seemed likely that Antonio's executive functioning problems related to the fact that he couldn't see or imagine or think about how the task would benefit him, he couldn't see what the payoff was going to be, and he couldn't work out how the task related to him and his ambitions.

It may have also been that Antonio had a strong preference for the known and a need for sameness in undertaking tasks in the classroom. Antonio had yet to become accustomed to change or the novelty of moving on and progressing to new tasks – in that situation, with that teacher and with those other students.

WANDERING OFF

Antonio had been inducted with his class group. We know that some people with autism have impairments of central coherence and as a result Antonio may not have been able to focus on whatever the teacher was expecting the students to be focused on. Had Antonio been explicitly and specifically instructed during the induction of that group to ensure that he was focusing on what was expected? Did Antonio know that the instructions being given by the teacher related to him? Had he been told that there were certain areas where he could *not* go. Because of central coherence impairments, we cannot assume that Antonio would have picked these things up automatically and his lack of compliance was the result of not realising that there were places that he was not allowed to enter. It was unclear how the information given to Antonio during the induction was presented and designed. There was mention of an 'induction pack', but none materialised.

GENERAL OBSERVATIONS

We know that people with autism are vulnerable to stress and anxiety as a consequence of not being able to understand the world around them. It was likely that in order to control his feelings of anxiety and confusion, Antonio's slamming doors, being disruptive in class and wandering off were ways of controlling both the situations he found himself in and the people around him (while also not appreciating the disturbance caused to them).

The consequences of his behaviours were to some extent always the same. We might say that he restored a degree of predictability and routine that had yet to be established.

The reasonable adjustments made

We have looked at how Antonio's presenting problems related to his autism. Now we must consider if Antonio was being treated *less favourably* compared to other students (the comparators) and if therefore he was being discriminated against?

There were a number of other students at the college for whom specific adjustments and adaptations had been made; these included ramps, support workers, signers, note takers and so on. There was nothing generally for people with autism (in terms of policy and procedure) nor was there anything specific for Antonio. So, yes. There was a strong likelihood that he *was* being discriminated against.

Initially the college wanted to provide a one-to-one support worker and since the funding mechanism for this via the Learning and Skills Council was well established, it seemed like an easy option, though an expensive one for the Treasury. However, through lengthy discussion and examination of the issues this was seen as unnecessary. Providing one-to-one support for students with complex needs in colleges is often a default response and in many cases serves only to police the student. 'Throwing people' at the problem was seen as not dealing with the underlying potentially discriminatory practice. It could have been argued that Antonio was still being discriminated against because he was autistic and that the college had still made no reasonable adjustments. The following strategies were arrived at.

SLAMMING DOORS

Any 'support' for Antonio at break times had stopped because the induction programme had finished. It was said, indeed the tick-box paperwork and evaluation reports and monitoring documents all illustrated, that the college and his tutors had considered that Antonio had passed his induction.

However, through discussion of autism and the kinds of impairments outlined in Chapter 1, it became clear that Antonio had not been given time to acclimatise to the new routine, and allow what he had been taught to bed in. Antonio's supervision during break had abruptly stopped, it had not been graduated at all and in many ways Antonio had suddenly been faced with a massive change in circumstances, again.

The college induction programme had not been designed to take into consideration individuals with autism, people who – because of their impairments – take a greater amount of time to acclimatise and adapt. This, it was decided, may have amounted to discrimination because the college was obliged to make reasonable adjustments and other students had had these made for them in order that they might complete their inductions successfully.

Alongside his existing classes, the college decided to rerun the induction for Antonio, this time allowing him more time to acclimatise to the various situations in which he would find himself and to become more accustomed to the routines of the timetable and the activities, including break times.

There was also now an understanding that Antonio had central coherence impairments and that this meant he may not have picked up that the instructions given during the induction to the group of students he was with were also for him. He may not have realised that the teacher meant him! As a result of this Antonio was explicitly shown again what *he* should be doing during the break time and the teacher (along with a number of helpful students in his group) modelled the appropriate behaviours and routines with *him* directly in situ. (Recall that it is important that people with autism are taught the skills they need in the situations where they will actually be using them.)

You might call this an individual, person-centred approach but someone else might not have had such a stark central coherence problem and therefore it would be unnecessary. If you tried to do it for every single student, it would become unmanageable, as many individualised programmes are.

Antonio was also given an illustrated micro timetable that had a clockface so he could manage the time he took to complete his activities during break time. After a few weeks Antonio got a feel for how long each activity took and the routine bedded in. His support tutor graduated his removal from supervising and teaching Antonio until he felt Antonio could do it himself. (This is the driving school approach to teaching. How do you know when a person is ready for their test and then drive on their own? You don't, it is not an exact art, and varies with each student.)

It was also explained to Antonio through the use of cartoons that he was damaging college property and that he would have to leave if he continued. There was some worry that he couldn't imagine (think about) this, that is he couldn't really see the consequences, so again visual presentations were made to him about calling the police if he continued banging the doors and being escorted off the premises by security. Antonio had enough understanding to be able to make use of this information. If he had not been able to, then calling the police might have been necessary (see the end of this section).

Note that there is not scope to deal with making reasonable adjustments for people with autism who have additional and severe challenging behaviours. Unravelling the complexities of the behaviours should really be considered only through taking consultations with the local support services – social workers, psychologists and others.

The danger with Antonio was that he might have stopped slamming doors but still been unable to manage break times and would perhaps start doing something else, possibly worse. He didn't and the slamming of doors stopped.

DISRUPTIVE IN CLASS

There is a wealth of information on supporting people with autism in the classroom which you can refer to (see Cumine *et al.* 1998; Howlin 1997; Jordan and Powell 1995). It is likely that many teachers nowadays already know much of this. In this instance the teacher was new and had not taught anyone with autism before. The teacher was informed about autism and the implications for teaching in a mixed class. (In fact a series of staff workshops for all teachers were held from which some of this case material arose.) The adjustments made included the following:

- Antonio was addressed directly so he knew that when the teacher was talking she also meant him.

- Visual cues and signposts meant that Antonio knew where he was at during the lesson.

- Tasks were broken down and sequenced.

- A set of classroom rules and a code of conduct was developed with the learners.

- The final goals, end result and end product were shown to Antonio so that he could see what he was aiming for and what the point of the lesson was.

- The teacher made reference to previous knowledge ensuring that Antonio could link information and tasks and see a connection. The teacher also developed a visual scheme of work, which was quite detailed and adapted from his own 'official' scheme of work (it became useful for other students too).

- The teacher decreased the use of abstract expressions and became more concrete in giving instructions, often giving Antonio separate instructions and alternative, but fair and relevant, ways to do the task.

- One of the most useful things to occur was that the teacher talked to the other students about Antonio and his autism and explained much of the above.

The effect was not instant and it took time for things to be absorbed, for a routine to be established and for Antonio to get into good habits.

There are many other adjustments that staff in further education colleges can make for students with autism. Antonio is only an example.

UNMOTIVATED BY MANY OF THE TASKS

The problems of motivation were overcome with the illustrated scheme of work and lesson plans through which Antonio could see where he was going. The lessons became more structured and consistent and he began to see what he was supposed to be doing, when and how.

WANDERING OFF

Once it was pointed out that Antonio had to be somewhere specific at a specific time and this became routine, he seemed to forget about wandering off. Remember in this scenario Antonio was not going to learn that he was in the wrong place and had gone absent without leave just from the looks on people's faces or by picking up the uncomfortable shuffling of the staff in Accounts and Finance.

Another student who had Asperger syndrome at the same college often wandered into prohibited areas largely because the staff in those areas would talk to him about his favourite subject – the local road system. In this instance he was told quite firmly but politely that the college security would call the police or he would be sent home if he persisted. (Security didn't take much notice again because he was a 'special needs' student.) This student knew he should not be in those areas, although it was felt that he may not have been aware of the seriousness of what he was doing: breaches of various Health and Safety policies etc. Despite being told on several occasions and in a variety of ways, he was twice sent home. He got the message. However, it also coincided with him being allowed to talk to a member of the learning support staff about his interest once a day for five minutes during his break. (I am unsure for how long this continued.) This was an excellent way of helping this student manage his specialist interest.

Jonathon

Brief description

Jonathon was 21 years old, had Asperger syndrome (a 'mild' form of autism) and had recently started working in a local government office. He had previously had a very successful work experience placement in his local library. Jonathon had attended mainstream school where he achieved four GCSEs. He went on to his local further education college gaining two Advanced levels. The Connexions careers officer from his schooldays had stayed in touch with Jonathon and through a series of formal and informal contacts had managed to help Jonathon with his CV, complete the application and then prepared him for interview. He got the job.

The job was as an administrative assistant and involved various clerical duties – maintaining files, disseminating information and documents to various different mailing lists, gathering information, photocopying, scanning images, collating reports and documents, sometimes taking telephone messages – all of which it was considered Jonathon was well suited to. While the employer knew that Jonathon had Asperger syndrome and had read a few leaflets, nothing else was considered necessary by way of support, information and guidance for either employer or employee. Problems began to occur immediately.

Presenting behaviours at work

JONATHON SOMETIMES COULDN'T GET INTO THE OFFICE

He would hover with his large bag and jacket outside in the corridor or by the lifts and seemed to be terrified of entering, though he always reported, when he was asked by other staff or security, that he was fine, rather bluntly. He attracted the attention of his supervisor, who, while always sympathetic, made Jonathon feel persecuted. Jonathon later reported that he felt everyone was looking at him, that he didn't think he was going to be able to do the work that he had to do that day, and that he thought other people in the office might pick on him or that he might make a mistake and then be sacked. These insecurities, anxieties and worries seemed to be constant and were extremely disabling.

JONATHON WOULDN'T ALWAYS DO THE WORK SET OR WOULD DO HIS OWN WORK

He seemed to find it difficult to get started on some of his work, he found deadlines nearly impossible and would sometimes drift off topic and do his own 'work'. Jonathon's own work consisted of recataloguing his collection of *Star Trek* videos and DVDs, his notebooks and photos. He would often take up, not only his own desk, but also any surfaces that had become vacant.

JONATHON WOULD MAKE MISTAKES AND THEN TRY TO FIX THEM HIMSELF

He made a whole range of mistakes that he attempted to fix himself, often then making the situation worse. Linked to this, he occasionally brought his own stationery into the office and was very protective of it. He once had a heated stand-up argument when a colleague borrowed his stapler.

JONATHON DIDN'T SEE THE NEED TO EXPLAIN THINGS TO OTHER PEOPLE

This included when he had finished something, when someone had left a message or he had discovered an error or noticed a mistake. He rarely talked to other people in the office and came across as chronically shy and inward. Once when he was being pursued by his supervisor and a colleague over some information about the work he had been doing, he hid!

JONATHON OFTEN TOOK UP A GREAT DEAL OF HIS SUPERVISOR'S TIME

For some tasks Jonathon could not work out what the expectations were of him when it came to making decisions or knowing what to do if it wasn't very obvious. He would often go to his supervisor. This was at first quite understandable. It was his supervisor's job to help him and make suggestions. But Jonathon's requests to be told what to do had become almost unmanageable and his supervisor found it increasingly difficult to cope with Jonathon's constant interruptions and enquiries.

COMMENT

Concerns quickly arose as to Jonathon's suitability for the job and after a number of informal meetings, he received a formal written warning. His supervisor commented: 'It's like he doesn't seem to *get it*.' Jonathon reported that he was afraid of things going wrong. He worried that everyone knew what to do so they must have had meetings without him. He reported that he couldn't see the point of coming in if he couldn't do the work. He told his supervisor that she was getting at him; he felt that she was picking on him and that being at work was worse than being at school.

How these behaviours relate to autism

People with autism do not walk around with a sign announcing their autism and it has been described by some as an 'invisible disability'. Because he is relatively bright, looks normal and has not had any 'special' schooling, for the most part it would be easy to overlook Jonathon's very real difficulties. However, the employer did know that Jonathon had Asperger syndrome and *the law has an expectation that employers take account of those with impairments such as autism and Asperger syndrome.*

COULDN'T GET INTO THE OFFICE

People with autism may avoid other people because they are afraid of them and because they find them difficult to predict. Jonathon was frightened to enter the office. He was unable to work out what everyone was doing, how he should react and what he should do if anyone spoke to him. It turned out that while he had been shown his desk, he had not been hosted into the office and shown around by someone. It was unfortunate that the day he started his supervisor was away and so since the first day, he had found it almost impossible to introduce himself to other people. These are largely theory of mind difficulties.

Jonathon may not have had much understanding that his behaviours affected how everyone else behaved towards him or what they thought of him. Seeing a connection between his behaviour and his ambitions to do the job and earn a living may have been difficult (central coherence difficulties). He may not have been able to regulate his fears and anxieties by himself and the impulse to avoid confronting what he didn't understand was strong.

We know that he may have had some problems undertaking new tasks and we can speculate that he may have had problems knowing how to approach the work he was going to be doing that day. It may have been difficult for him to imagine how his day might be OK and without problems and so reduce his avoiding behaviours (executive functioning problems).

Jonathon reported being persecuted by questions from his supervisor. Because of the theory of mind impairment in people with autism, it is possible that Jonathon did not understand the role of his supervisor or that of the other staff. Without being explicitly told that it was the job of his supervisor to tell him what to do, monitor his work and give feedback that he needed to act on, he would not easily have picked this up. The same may be true for his relationship with other employees.

Reading the motives and intentions of others is fraught with difficulties and it would seem that Jonathon was the sort of person who may have avoided his colleagues because he could not 'read' them. It may have also been the case that while Jonathon had seen his job description and understood his duties these may not have included, at least not very explicitly included, how he should interact with his colleagues and what his role was in relation to his supervisor.

People with autism can take time to acclimatise to new people, new experiences and situations and new tasks; it was unclear if he had had much induction or training. His previous work experience record belied the fact that this job was a brand new situation and there were assumptions that Jonathon would transfer his abilities from school and the work at the local library to the local government offices.

WOULDN'T DO WORK SET OR WOULD DO HIS OWN WORK

A lack of compliance is brought about because of central coherence difficulties. The person with autism does not draw together the various cues in the environment and from the signals of people around them in order to know how to behave. They may not feel the embarrassment nor be able to read the signals of disapproval from other people and so in some respects do not fully appreciate that what they are doing is not quite right for the situation they are in.

Should the task he was undertaking not be clear enough, it may be that his ability to focus on it is difficult. Common sense tells us that his job description would not need to have included a clause that said you are not allowed to indulge your hobbies while at work. Personnel will have assumed that people generally pick up how to do their jobs and what is 'appropriate' from the culture and the climate of the environment in which those jobs are conducted. This was something that in retrospect should have been dealt with immediately rather than have been allowed to have drifted.

Problems of planning, starting and finishing relate to impairments of executive functioning, and anxieties about getting the task right (perfect) rather than done satisfactorily arise as a result of not being able to see the whole picture (impairments of central coherence).

WOULD MAKE MISTAKES AND THEN TRY TO FIX THEM

Not understanding that other people can be helpful is a theory of mind problem. In this instance Jonathon didn't ask for help because he thought that by making a mistake, he had done something wrong and he would get into trouble. The sort of information about what you do if you make a mistake is usually hidden somewhere in the ambiance and culture of the workplace and not usually the subject of explicit policy or information, not a run of the mill mistake anyway. To some of us it's just obvious that mistakes occur; to someone with autism it is not and, because of impairments in central coherence and theory of mind, neither are people with autism likely to just 'pick it up'.

Not picking up that the office would supply him with stationery also relates to impairments in the central coherence. Not making use of other people and not seeing other people as a source of information are theory of mind impairments. The preservative nature of autism, that is how a person will make the same mistake over and over and not learn from their experiences (remember the sweet in the box?), may have affected Jonathon.

DIDN'T SEE THE NEED TO EXPLAIN THINGS

If you do not see that other people have minds of their own (theory of mind) and do not think the same things as you do, there may not be any reason to report information you have to those people. Jonathon may not have known nor been able to work out that other people need to know the things that he knew. With Jonathon it may well also have been the case that he lacked some practice in knowing *how* to address and approach other people to report things that he was thinking or concerned about and so compounded his problems. And this was not something he could have worked out. These are impairments in executive functioning.

His lack of experience and that he was never actually taught or shown how he should report or explain things was also a probable factor in his failings as an employee. Jonathon would have found it quite difficult to picture himself in the situation, hold on to this image or thought and then choreograph himself in a future position discussing with someone something that has happened in the past.

TOOK UP A GREAT DEAL OF HIS SUPERVISOR'S TIME

Jonathon seems to have found it difficult to read the expectations of his supervisor. He also found it hard to pick up the extent to which he needed to ask for help or the extent to which he should seek clarification when he didn't know what to do. Once Jonathon had got into the habit of always asking his supervisor's opinion rather than thinking for himself it was difficult to shake.

GENERAL OBSERVATIONS

It should be clear at this point in what ways Jonathon's impairments along with a lack of explicit information between people in the workplace created these difficulties. We would no longer consider that it was a wheelchair user's 'fault' that they were unable to use stairs; we would provide level access or a lift. It is the same for people with autism.

One day Jonathon's supervisor shouted at him: 'Have I got to point out absolutely everything to you!?' To which Jonathon simply and calmly replied: 'Yes.'

The reasonable adjustments made

We saw in Chapter 2 that the law obliges an employer or shopkeeper or educational establishment to take reasonable steps to prevent disadvantage through making *reasonable adjustments*. What is *reasonable* will depend on a number of factors including costs, disruption and resources. We have had this in mind when considering what might be considered reasonable.

It is for the employer, school or service provider to take a view as to what they think is reasonable (and take into account the Guidance, Code of Practice and so on) but ultimately a court decides. However, it is accepted that there are a range of reasonable responses and as long as you are within the range, you are legal.

COULDN'T GET INTO THE OFFICE

Jonathon was given a brief explanation of what people would be doing each day and how this related to his role. His supervisor made up a detailed timetable of the tasks he would be expected to do as far as was possible. Jonathon was also told that occasionally he would be approached by another member of staff who would ask him to do something but that they would also try to tell him when it should be done by.

Jonathon's supervisor painted a picture of Jonathon's work going well. She described to him what his day would be like and what would happen and what to do if people say hello and what he should do about his hobbies if he felt compelled to do them. Jonathon was also supervised more closely (which bettered the relationship he developed with his supervisor).

Jonathon was given more time to get used to the idea of new tasks and again as far as was possible, they weren't just sprung on him, he was given some notice. In fact what happened was that people started to say things like: 'I'm sorry Jonathon but I am going to have to spring this on you rather suddenly.' Not always those words of course but using this phrase gave Jonathon time to prepare himself for the shock and novelty of being given new information about what he was supposed to be doing.

Jonathon also worked out for himself that if he got into work before other people arrived, he wouldn't be so anxious. Jonathon was shown what to do if he did make a mistake and what the procedure was should a mistake occur.

WOULDN'T DO WORK SET OR WOULD DO HIS OWN WORK

He was given immediate feedback about the consequences of not reporting that he was having difficulties getting on with a piece of work. Where his own 'work' was concerned it was explained to him in ways he would not misunderstand that he simply couldn't undertake his hobbies while at work, which he accepted.

Jonathon was given examples and, where needed, demonstrations of any new tasks. Over time he developed a bank of experiences that he could draw on. If he didn't know how to tackle something it was pointed out that he needed to explain as well as he could what the problems he was having were so that someone else might be able to help. Some tasks were broken down into time-scales and smaller units so that he could manage his time more effectively.

WOULD MAKE MISTAKES AND DIDN'T SEE THE NEED TO EXPLAIN THINGS

It was explained to Jonathon why there was a need to explain things to other people. There was some debate about what exactly he needed to explain (lest there was a danger he would explain everything). It was decided that his supervisor would go through a series of 'what to do if' scenarios for common problems that she thought might arise.

Over time he also got used to the idea that setbacks did occur and happened to other people too. In many ways Jonathon needed to be able to do the job and make mistakes before anyone would be able to see how his impairments would impact on his ability to do the work.

TOOK UP A GREAT DEAL OF HIS SUPERVISOR'S TIME

Jonathon's supervisor began to be clearer with Jonathon about the expectations involved in a task, that is what components of the job he was expected to be able to think about and make decisions about himself without always making reference to his supervisor.

If Jonathon had not been able to make some decisions for himself without making reference to his supervisor all of the time, it is unlikely that he would have been seen to be competent in being able to do the job and that any reasonable adjustments such as being told what to do all the time may have been seen to be unreasonable.

Hindsight is often the key to reasonable adjustments and it is difficult to predict or make environments autism friendly when everyone with autism is different and would react differently to different environments and different people.

Importantly for Jonathon, other employees were told about Asperger syndrome and given some indication of the best ways to communicate with him and also some explanation for what had happened.

In hindsight

See further discussion at the end of the chapter. Adaptations could have been made to the interview process to elicit any problems. Jonathon could have been given a trial week in which to identify support needs and certainly his induction could have been delegated to someone else in his supervisor's absence. Much more about what the job involved could have been made explicit in his job description (after all they had translated it into Braille; there was no reason not to make it autism friendly too – as far as might be possible).

Jonathon also needed to make some changes: he was taught more about his Asperger syndrome and in what ways it affected him and how this affected his ability to do his job. He was also taught what he could say to other people about autism and what he could say about the adjustments that an employer may need to make for him – within reason.

Janet

Brief description

Janet was different from Jonathon and Antonio. She was 18 and diagnosed as having autism and severe learning difficulties. She had been to a special school, then to a specialist residential college and had returned to her home in London. After a brief time at her parents' home without anything to do, she was found a place in a large mixed day centre for people with learning difficulties.

Reports from the residential college stated that she could follow the daily routine, make her own way to the canteen, carry out basic daily tasks such as washing up, laying the table, shopping at a supermarket, loading a washing machine and that she was continent and could use public transport. Janet, the reports stated, could make her needs known through some basic Makaton sign language.

There was little reference to reports of what Janet was like before going to the college, although some of the school reports suggested that prior to leaving school, Janet had become very anxious and had started losing many of the skills that she had learnt and that she would need an 'autism-friendly environment' in order to function effectively.

The day centre reported that Janet could do none of the things outlined in the college report and that the staff were unhappy with the disruption she had caused to the existing users and their routines. The staff suggested that the day centre was not the most appropriate placement for Janet and that Janet would not be able to learn to take part as the centre was too complex and not an 'autism environment'. This sounded as if Janet was about to lose her place on the grounds of her disability and there was a likelihood that this would amount to discrimination.

UNIVER... ...NCHESTER
LIBRARY

Janet's parents were keen to have Janet stay somewhere local but were equally aware that neither Janet nor the day centre were happy with the current arrangements. Janet's uncertain time at the day centre coincided with the manager organising a training day on autism.

As soon as the staff were told that people with autism do not transfer or generalise knowledge and skills easily, the subject of Janet came up. Applying knowledge about autism (Chapter 1) to Janet, the staff began to think that everything Janet had 'learnt' at the specialist residential college was no longer relevant to the day centre; it had been relevant only to the college. The residential college had taught Janet the skills she needed to attend *that* college, use the local public transport in *that* area only, lay a *specific* table at a *specific* time with people she had got to know and she had got used to. They also suspected that Janet had got into the habit of taking herself to the toilet within the routines of *that* college.

They also realised that the Makaton signing was being used within a specific context and that it was possible that she signed at the college only after she had got into the habit of it and the use of Makaton had become embedded in the routines of her daily life at the college.

It became obvious that Janet had been expected to be able to use the skills she had learnt at the college to the day centre. Without anyone having to do anything, it was expected that she would pick up on the existing routines and fit into them since this is what was reported she could do at the college.

Presenting behaviours at the day centre

In this section we list the problems Janet and the day centre faced. Problems began to occur from day one, and included the following:

- Janet had no formal speech. She had echolalia, made 'blocking noises' and did not use Makaton, though she did copy the sign others made when she was being addressed.

- It was said that Janet was incontinent, though she was not at home. This was extremely distressing and disruptive to Janet, the staff and other users. Because of her incontinence staff didn't feel she could go out on public transport or to the local shops.

- She would sit at a desk but not undertake any tasks. At lunchtimes she would be reluctant to sit with the other students and eat lunch. (Lunchtimes were usually relaxed, freeform affairs where some people went to a café or brought sandwiches and other bought-in packed lunches.)

- Janet would wander off and often force her way out of a room in which she was supposed to be doing an activity, barging through people and flaying about on the floor if she couldn't get her way.

- She needed constant prompting to do anything and most of the time did nothing.

- Janet spent much of her time pacing up and down in the same spot, reacting badly when approached by turning away and growling.

- Most of her behaviours were described as 'inappropriate'.

How these behaviours relate to autism

Put simply, Janet had all the triad of impairments and met the criteria of the ICD-10 and DSM-IV which we looked at in some detail in Chapter 1. Janet experienced three main areas of difficulty, the triad of impairments:

- social impairments: difficulty with social relationships and interacting with other people

- communication: difficulty with verbal and non-verbal communication

- imagination: difficulty in the development of play and imagination and the ability to think about things along with rigid and repetitive behaviours and routines.

It should be pointed out that understanding and making sense of these behaviours is difficult and takes time and a lot of effort. Janet benefited from a staff group who, while quick to make judgements based on the information provided to them from the college, were able to rapidly adapt and think creatively about how to make changes in what they were doing: *reasonable adjustments.*

At the day centre Janet's impairments had become chronic disabilities, because the day centre (although they had other people with autism attending) was not a particularly autism-friendly environment.

The reasonable adjustments made

The day centre was reminded that there was a good case that Janet was being discriminated against: she was being treated less favourably as there were no reasonable adjustments in place for her, whereas there were for other centre users.

We should remind ourselves that the Disability Discrimination Act imposes a legal obligation on employers, schools and service providers to make *reasonable adjustments* so that the 'disabled person', the person with autism, is not put at a substantial disadvantage, as compared to other users. This is not about 'inclusion'.

There was much discussion about teaching Janet the social and communicative skills that she would need in the day centre: a social skills programme was to include turn-taking, friendship and citizenship skills along with teaching her to use Makaton. These were all very noble suggestions and were suggested with the best intentions.

However, it was pointed out that not only would locating the difficulty solely within the individual be seen as discrimination but also it was unlikely that Janet, who had been in education for some 13 years, would have the facilities to learn things that she had been formally diagnosed as being unable to do. 'Whatever strategies are employed to improve social functioning, it important to recognise that the fundamental deficits are likely to remain throughout life' (Howlin 1997, p.87). As Patricia Howlin goes on to point out, it is the flexibility and ability of others to adapt that is often more important.

The first thing the day centre did was to assume that whatever Janet did she would need time to acclimatise. There were strong visual cues or illustrations of instructions, activities that were relevant, large and practical, and the centre set up a regular written timetable and installed a number of set activities.

There were side benefits to other users of the centre who, while they had got used to arriving each day and waiting to see what was going to happen and were very willing to 'see how the day feels' and do 'what we fancy doing', benefited from this new more organised, structured approach. There was little resistance among staff since they could see that they had legal obligations to make changes: reasonable adjustments.

The centre designed its own version of a schedule outlined in Patricia Howlin's book *Autism* (1997) and originally devised by Schuler *et al.* (1989). The staff initially focused on finding out in what ways Janet let people know what she wanted and how she communicated her needs. Her parents were also asked to give some insight; in fact Janet's father, who had retired, spent time at the centre with Janet and in a sense facilitated the transferring of what she could do at home to the centre. The knowledge of parents about their own children cannot be underestimated.

The day centre labelled all the cupboards and drawers and put symbols on doors so that Janet could 'read' where things were. (The problem with this is that the symbol is not the thing itself and Janet may not have been able to hold in mind the symbol and think about that to which it relates.) People with autism can usually locate things in cupboards and know what rooms are used for out of habit. They might not always be able to 'read' the labels and symbols on the cupboard doors. Janet could match and so she was given a picture she could match to another of the same. Again there were significant benefits to other users.

Many of the difficult to manage behaviours of other people who attended the centre improved. There were increased levels of independence and less need for chaperoning of users around – over time they all knew where they needed to go and when. The use of agency staff decreased and financially the centre was better off. Staff were clearer about their roles, communications between staff and users improved and it appeared that the skill levels of the users also rose.

Through a strong manager and committed staff, the centre made sure (as far as was possible) that the day was structured and full of routine and that everything was the same, happened at the same time and with the same people – as far as was practical of course. They could not avoid change, nor could they avoid Janet becoming anxious when things didn't fall into line; they did strike a happy medium however.

It took four months for Janet just to become acclimatised to staying in a room with other people, sitting at a table and undertaking an activity. She was not expected to sit at a desk for very long and activities were always large: shopping, cooking, put things away, some gardening, washing up and cleaning table tops.

She became continent because she was always taken to the toilets at set times; after three months or so she began to take herself and she did learn to associated the Makaton sign of toilet with the action of going to the toilet. Janet would always need to take time to get used to new staff and new activities but if the routine was the same she would be less anxious.

Conclusions

Janet was typical of what happens to many people with autism who go away to residential schools or colleges. You may well know about the gap between how a child behaves or performs at school and how they behave and perform at home. Many schools do not address this gap as part of what might be considered to be 'appropriate learning for people with autism'. This of course is a shame because it means that many children with autism are unable to generalise the skills that they have at home to school or that they have at school to home. This practice might be considered discriminatory if it weren't for the fact that many of these schools don't have a programme of ensuring skills are useful for students outside of those schools, for *any* of their learners.

Likewise, many residential colleges do not recruit locally and so whatever their students with autism learn is – and this is blunt – wasted on them. Once those students leave the residential college – and some get 'fed through the system to the residential units' so that they never leave – but if they do, most colleges do not have systems and resources in place where those skills can be generalised back home. The main bus route through the city of Bristol is just not the same as one in a commuter town such as Haywards Heath.

Autism, reasonable adjustments and the law

What can we learn from the case studies? First, however odd it looks, if the person has a formal diagnosis, then it is likely that the person with autism finds understanding other people and the world around extremely difficult to manage. As a result of these impairments in the hard-wiring of their brains, people with autism do have relatively 'odd' behaviours. It should also be noted that because of this hard-wiring people with autism are better disposed than the rest of us for certain jobs and excel in areas where their autism is an asset: jobs which involve having a narrow focus of attention, an ability to pick out detail and focus on a singular task and that involve a degree of logic.

Second, we should remind ourselves that there is now a new law which says quite simply that you cannot discriminate against people with autism and that saying that you do not have the facilities or resources to 'support' or 'cater for the needs' of someone with autism, without having considered making reasonable adjustments, is against the law.

If this has happened to you, if you think that your child has been or is being discriminated against – and one only needs to read the local papers and follow the news on various websites to see this is the case – then you can now take legal action against the employer, college or service from which your son or daughter has been refused access, if it's solely on the grounds of their autism.

We have seen that people with autism need very different reasonable adjustments from those for people with other impairments. However, the sorts of adjustments people with autism need might often benefit everyone, for example:

- explicit information

- clear expectations

- structure, routine, habit

- consistency

- time to acclimatise.

These are large generalisations and each individual with autism will be different.

Providing reasonable adjustments in colleges

Most colleges will be well aware of their duties under the DDA and the 2007 Code of Practice issued by the former Disability Rights Commission

(DRC) for post-16 education. This section, along with Chapter 4, is meant to provide additional information not covered in that code. The DRC Code of Practice states:

> The duty to make reasonable adjustments is a cornerstone of the Act and requires education providers to take positive steps to ensure that disabled people can access education and related services. This goes beyond simply avoiding treating disabled people less favourably and in some cases it may also mean taking additional steps to which non-disabled people are not entitled. Many reasonable adjustments are inexpensive and in some cases Disabled Students' Allowances or other funding will be available to cover some of the costs. (Disability Rights Commission 2007)

The duty is also anticipatory and colleges must now make plans to be able to provide reasonable adjustment to future students. Colleges should be constantly seeking ways to make reasonable adjustments. While there are three mentions of reasonable adjustments for people with autism in the code, there are many more that need to be considered and may not be obvious; this section will help to highlight these.

There is some repetition between this section and the next on employment. This section is also relevant to schools and day centres.

Enrolment and application

It would be helpful if information being targeted at students with autism were designed to be clear, unfussy and straightforward. Any advertisement on advertising materials using abstract symbolic language, such as 'Enrol now! Stop dreaming: reach your potential', is unlikely to be easily understood by someone with autism.

> *Not providing clear language, free of abstractions, in pre-enrolment information could be seen as discriminatory.*

Induction

Any induction should cover the social aspects of using the college, not how to make friends but how to use the canteen, what the rules about behaviour are and the codes of conduct that are expected. Importantly students with autism will need to be given more time than many other students in order for them to acclimatise and get used to new routines and tasks, new people and situations. Good habits need to be established from the beginning.

Not providing the student with autism time to acclimatise through the induction into the college environment, with the various people they will interact with, could be seen as discrimination.

Interview

Interviews are difficult for many people with autism. Given the impairments of autism, a person would find answering questions about themselves and being asked to speculate on their abilities in a future situation extremely hard. Reasonable adjustments to an interview might include the following:

- asking closed rather than open questions

- asking questions that are about a student's concrete experiences at school or that relate specifically to skills and interests of the student

- allowing the student to prepare for interview by disclosing the questions to be asked a few days beforehand

- avoid hypothetical or abstract language: 'How would you go about...?' and 'If you were in a situation where...'

- letting the student know when they have given the required information and enough of it

- rewording questions using less abstract language and where the person with autism may interpret questions literally.

A student with autism was unable to attend for an interview because he was worried what it might be like. A member of teaching staff met the potential student at his careers adviser's office and showed him a series of photographs which included students at the college working, the office where the interview was to be held, the car park and other pictures of the college including other staff he might meet. A week later he was being interviewed at the college and then a term later he was attending.

Not adapting the interview to provide more concrete ways of eliciting information from a student could be seen to be discriminatory.

Structure

Students with autism will need to know what they are doing, when they are doing it and with whom. Learning materials and resources should be well organised and where appropriate be consistently available. (Where materials are moved regularly, someone with autism may not spontaneously go off and start looking for them and enquiring from other people as to where the materials they need have gone.) A clear timetable of activities should be considered the equivalent of a wheelchair for someone who has no use of their legs. Students will often need help organising their work things and help in planning how they will manage their workloads. Recall that these are real impairments of executive functioning and people with autism find pulling the various pieces of information together so that they can organise and plan a series of actions very difficult (and not in the same ways that other people might).

Not providing an organised, well-structured, consistent environment, especially in class, is highly likely to result in accusations of discrimination.

What does this mean? Things such as using the same rooms, having consistent staffing, being clear about what the task is, making sure there is a programme of lessons and that the outcomes are clear. This will of course vary with subjects.

People with autism will need reasonable adjustments during unstructured times such as breaks and lunch. They will not be able to know what to do with themselves without being shown and may need suggestions as to what they can do, such as read a magazine or a book: this will vary enormously according to each student. Hosting circumstances where two or more people with autism could join together or finding other people within the school or college that have similar interests as the person with autism could also be hugely beneficial.

Making things explicit

Unwritten rules, codes of conduct and how people know how to interact will be alien to people with autism and they certainly will not pick them up.

> *A failure to set boundaries by members of staff would be seen to be discrimination since the person with autism cannot see for themselves where those boundaries would be needed.*

For any college staff with promiscuous attitudes toward the behaviours of students, this should be noted.

Feedback

People with autism will find it difficult to pick up social and interpersonal cues around them and may assume that their performance is acceptable unless told otherwise. Teaching staff need to be able to provide well-timed and completely explicit non-judgemental feedback and not assume the student with autism has done something deliberately or wilfully wrong.

During feedback provide examples of alternatives (if needed) to the problem at hand; expectations about performance should also be made explicit.

> *A failure to provide timely feedback to a student about their behaviour could result in accusations of discrimination.*

Teaching instructions, guidance and expectations

Clear instruction and guidance about expectations that would normally be unwritten need to be made available to the student with autism: this is essential. When giving instructions or explanations, it is necessary to be concise, specific and often graphic (put it in writing). Do not assume the student will 'get it', that is that they will be able to infer and pick up what you think might have been obvious. (Recall the example of asking the student to post the letter!)

Sometimes it will be a reasonable adjustment to break a large task up into its component steps. Students with autism experience a great deal of anxiety and stress when they cannot see how they are going to manage a task or a requirement. They cannot always 'see' how they are going to cope with an activity that seems to them to be overwhelming. The task, where possible, should also be structured so that the beginning, middle and end are clear. Often, and teachers do this naturally, check that the student has understood, but not just what to do; check they have understood *how* they should be doing it.

Auxiliary information

A useful tool for some students with autism and Asperger syndrome at further education colleges and in mainstream schools is creating a document, booklet, file, notebook or filofax insert etc. that contains useful information related to the 'social' and 'relating' aspects of the environment – a kind of cue card or reference handbook. In the future no doubt this sort of information can be implanted into everyone's head and we will all have access to the Internet and auxiliary information when we need it. Another person with autism made the observation to me when discussing Antonio that the teacher had become part of the task and that while a graduated approach was a good idea, a better one for higher functioning people with autism was 'an auxiliary mind'. This might avoid students getting stuck or becoming over-reliant on checking everything with a teacher (we saw this with Jonathon and his supervisor). Students can be taught to make reference to their notebook rather than having to ask the same questions about things that have already been explained.

A student handbook, especially one for a student with autism, can also be illustrated and should contain information that would normally be picked up by non-autistic students.

> *Not providing the student with auxiliary information – a notebook – about things that non-autistic people will automatically pick up and indeed are expected to pick up, could be seen as discrimination.*

Such a notebook might also include the kinds of things that can and cannot be talked about especially where someone with autism says or does something inappropriate (for example, Jonathon not realising that he could not undertake his hobby at work). These can obviously only be suggestive and will never be exhaustive but can go some way in assisting some people with autism in understanding the unwritten rules of a school or college.

Disciplinary procedures

The student with autism is not going to understand disciplinary procedures that are written in an abstract language and if the information is not accessible to someone with autism, the college may be accused of discrimination. Teachers should always bear in mind whether the student with autism who has breached any code of practice fully understands what has happened and how they are in breach of any school or college rules.

Note that it is highly unlikely that many people with autism would be able to manage a 'mixed package' of education or care – a little bit of this and a little bit of that. It is unlikely that people with autism would manage easily on part-time courses when the rest of the week they are unable to occupy their time.

> *Because of the impairments of executive function and central coherence it may now be considered discriminatory if colleges and schools cannot organise the delivery of their courses to learners with Autistic Spectrum Disorders.*

There is a great deal more to be said for making reasonable adjustments for people with autism within schools and colleges and this section of the chapter has introduced some of the basic ways in which teachers can make reasonable adjustments and should set teachers thinking about particular students in their charge.

We now turn to employers.

Providing reasonable adjustments at work

Most employers will be well aware of their duties under the DDA and the former Disability Rights Commission's Code of Practice, in which autism is mentioned four times. There is some considerable overlap between this section and the previous. If you are a teacher this section may not be relevant to you, although if you are organising work experience or you are a careers officer it will be.

Employers, careers advisers, disability employment advisers, personnel officers and human resources staff should read the section in Chapter 2 on the Hewett v. Motorola Ltd. In this case an employee with autism made a number of complaints to an employment tribunal while he was employed alleging disability discrimination. He claimed that his employer had failed to provided adequate training, supervision and support, had failed to make reasonable adjustments to employment policies and procedures, and had discriminated against him in the way that it had monitored his performance in his appraisal.

This section will use the same format as in the previous section on reasonable adjustments for colleges. For more information about employing people with autism, see the conclusion to this volume, which gives an example of an excellent scheme that helps employers make reasonable adjustments.

Advertisements and applications

It is unlikely that any advertisement or advertising materials using abstract symbolic language will be easily understood by someone with autism.

> Not providing clear information and language, free of abstractions, on application forms could be seen as discriminatory.

Interview

Interviews are difficult for many people with autism. Given the impairments of autism, a person would find answering questions about themselves and being asked to speculate on their abilities in a future situation extremely hard. For an employer it is important to know a person can do the job. Allowing someone with autism to do the job, as part of the interview process, may be considered a reasonable adjustment.

Reasonable adjustments to an interview might include the following:

- asking closed rather than open questions

- asking questions that are about an applicant's concrete experiences at school or that relate specifically to skills and interests of the applicant

- allowing the applicant to prepare for interview by disclosing the questions to be asked a few days beforehand

- avoiding hypothetical or abstract language: 'How would you go about…?' and 'If you were in a situation where…'

- letting the applicant know when they have given the required information and answered the question

- rewording questions using less abstract language and where the person with autism may interpret questions literally.

Not adapting the interview to provide more concrete ways of eliciting information from an applicant could be seen to be discriminatory.

Induction and training

Any induction should cover the social aspects of using the workplace, not how to make friends but how to use the canteen, what the rules about behaviour are and the codes of conduct that are expected. Importantly employees with autism will need to be given more time than many other employees in order for them to acclimatise and get used to new routines and tasks, new people and situations. Good habits need to be established from the beginning.

Not providing the employee with autism time to acclimatise through the induction into the work environment, with the various people they will interact with, could be seen as discrimination.

Structure

Employees with autism will need to know what they are doing, when they are doing it and with whom. Materials and resources should be well organised and where appropriate be consistently available. (Where materials are moved regularly, someone with autism may not spontaneously go off and start looking for them and enquiring from other people as to where the materials they need have gone.) A clear timetable of tasks, activities and responsibilities should be considered the equivalent of a wheelchair for someone who has no use of their legs. Employees will often need help organising their work things and help in planning how they will manage their workloads. Recall that these are real impairments of executive functioning and people with autism find pulling the various pieces of information together so that they can organise and planning a series of actions very difficult (and not in the same ways that other people might).

Not providing an organised well-structured environment, especially in the workplace, is highly likely to result in accusations of discrimination.

What it means to be organised and structured will vary but might include using the same rooms, having consistent meetings and briefs, being clear about what the task is, making sure there is programme of work and that the outcomes are clear. This will of course vary with each job.

Employees with autism will need reasonable adjustments during unstructured times such as breaks and lunch. They will not be able to know what to do with themselves without being shown and may need suggestions as to what they can do, such as read a magazine or a book: this will vary enormously according to each employee.

Making things explicit

Unwritten rules, codes of conduct and how people know how to interact will be alien to people with autism and they certainly will not pick them up.

> *A failure to set boundaries by management could be seen to be discrimination since the person with autism cannot see for themselves where those boundaries would be needed.*

Feedback

Employees with autism will find it difficult to pick up social and interpersonal cues around them and may assume that their performance is acceptable unless told otherwise. Supervising staff need to be able to provide well-timed and completely explicit non-judgemental feedback and not assume the employee with autism has done something deliberately or wilfully wrong.

During feedback, alternatives (if needed) to the problem at hand should be given and expectations about performance should be made explicit.

> *A failure to provide timely feedback to an employee about their behaviour could result in accusations of discrimination.*

Instructions, job descriptions, guidance and expectations

Clear instructions and job descriptions along with guidance about expectations that would normally be unwritten need to be made available to the employee with autism: this is essential. The words 'And anything else deemed within the spirit and scope of this job description' is not good enough. When giving instructions or explanations, it is necessary to be concise, specific and often graphic (put it in writing). Do not assume the employee will 'get it', that is that they will be able to infer and pick up what you think might have been obvious. (Recall the example of asking the student to post the letter!)

Sometimes it will be a reasonable adjustment to break a large task up into its component steps. Employees with autism experience a great deal of anxiety and stress when they cannot see how they are going to manage a task or a requirement. They cannot always 'see' how they are going to cope with an activity that seems to them to be overwhelming. The task, where possible, should also be structured so that any beginning, middle and end is clear. Often, and most supervisors or managers will do this naturally, check that the employee has understood, but not just what to do; check they have understood how they should be doing it.

Auxiliary information

A useful tool for some students with autism and Asperger syndrome at work or on work experience placements is creating a document, booklet, file, notebook or filofax insert etc. that contains useful information related to the 'social' and 'relating' aspects of the environment – a kind of cue card or reference handbook. A notebook will avoid an employee with autism getting stuck or becoming over-reliant on checking everything with a supervisor (we saw this with Jonathon and his boss). Employees can be taught to make reference to their notebook rather than having to ask the same questions about things that have already been explained.

An employee handbook, especially one for an employee with autism, can also be illustrated and should contain information that would normally be picked up by non-autistic employees.

> *Not providing the employee with auxiliary information – a notebook – about things that non-autistic people will automatically pick up and indeed are expected to pick up, could be seen as discrimination.*

Such a notebook might also include the kinds of things that can and cannot be talked about especially where someone with autism says

UNIVERSITY OF WINCHESTER
LIBRARY

something highly inappropriate (recall the social worker about whom a student said: 'Wow, aren't you fat!' in Chapter 1 and Jonathon not realising that he could not undertake his hobby at work). These can obviously only be suggestive and will never be exhaustive but can go some way in assisting some people with autism in understanding the unwritten rules of a workplace.

Information and training for staff and other employees

In Chapter 2 we saw that:

> In some cases a reasonable adjustment will not work without the cooperation of other employees. Employees may therefore have an important role in helping to ensure a reasonable adjustment is carried out in practice.

And specifically for autistic employees the Code of Practice indicated that:

> It is a reasonable adjustment for an employee to communicate in a particular way to an employee with autism (a disability which can make it difficult for someone to understand normal social interaction among people). As part of the reasonable adjustment it is the responsibility of that employer to seek the co-operation of other employees in communicating in that way.

Giving other employees information on disabilities generally is probably a good idea and organisations such as the National Autistic Society in the UK or the National Autistic Societies of Wales and Scotland will be able to help with this.

Where possible it is useful for the employee with autism to have some knowledge of how autism affects them and you can get calling cards with information about autism on them that can be very useful for employees to hand out when needed. (Chapter 4 also points out an employment scheme where help for employers in making reasonable adjustments can be found.)

Disciplinary procedures

The employee with autism is not going to understand disciplinary procedures that are written in an abstract language and if the information is not accessible to someone with autism, the company may be accused of discrimination. Managers should always bear in mind whether the employee with autism who has breached any code of practice fully understands what has happened and how they are in breach of any workplace rules.

There is a great deal more to be said for making reasonable adjustments for people with autism within workplaces and this section of the chapter has introduced some of the basic ways in which employers and managers can make reasonable adjustments and should set them thinking about particular employees in their charge.

The kinds of work a person with an Autistic Spectrum Disorder can do

The jobs and tasks for which people with autism are best suited will vary in the same way that how their impairments affect each individual personality will also vary. Jobs that can coincide with the interests of a person will obviously be ideal.

The sorts of jobs that people with autism may be well disposed to because of their impairments include:

- jobs where attention to detail and accuracy is required

- jobs involving numbers, statistics and facts

- tasks where there is a clear procedure to follow

- structured environments and activities with defined procedures.

People with autism usually have the following attributes:

- being able to concentrate on one particular task for lengthy periods

- reliability

- accuracy (often 100 per cent)

- close attention to detail and an ability to identify errors

- technical ability (many have excellent information technology skills and qualifications)

- detailed factual knowledge (often encyclopedic)

- excellent memory

- conscientiousness and persistence.

The National Autistic Society Employment Scheme – Prospects (which will be discussed more in the Conclusion to this book) points out:

> It is commonly thought that because people with an ASD [autistic spectrum disorder] typically experience problems with communication, social interaction and changes in routine, they are unlikely to do well in jobs which require these skills. However, while many people with an ASD don't feel comfortable in environments where there are unexpected changes, or in jobs which involve a lot of face-to-face with customers, there are others who thrive in these roles, including some in senior positions. Prospects has supported people with an ASD taking on jobs such as tour assistant, project leader and after school club worker, all of which involve a high level of communication and adaptation. (National Autistic Society 2004, p.4)

4

Reference Table

Introduction

Once again, let us remind ourselves of what we mean by a *reasonable adjustment*. The Disability Discrimination Act imposes an obligation on employers, schools and service providers to make reasonable adjustments so that the person with disabilities is not put at a substantial disadvantage, as compared to a non-disabled person. If the arrangements for admission to the schools or the policy or practice of an employer or service provider mean that the person with disabilities is placed at a substantial disadvantage, then reasonable steps must be taken to address that disadvantage.

It is not possible to prescribe what amounts to reasonable adjustments in every potential situation that could arise. The former Disability Rights Commission has developed codes of practice which tribunals and courts must have regard to. These give an ideal of the sorts of adjustments that could be made. This could include reallocating duties, redeployment, changing working hours, providing special equipment, providing supervision or support. This chapter is a contribution to those codes of practice.

What follows is only a *guide* and it should be remembered that not all of the behaviours of a person with autism would be the result of autism-related 'impairments'. The list is by no means exhaustive and where a problem persists and it is unclear what kinds of reasonable adjustments should be made then a further expertise should be sought.

There is some repetition throughout the reference table, where we shall be looking again at:

- triad of impairments

- theory of mind

- central coherence

- executive functioning.

Summary

In the preface to this volume we stated that people with autism were different from people with other types of impairments. Most other people have impairments in physical abilities. People with autism have impairments in their social and relating abilities and you will be well aware of the many ways in which people with autism differ from people with other kinds of impairments. Indeed you may now be more aware of the kinds of things that people with autism have *in common* with other members of the population, especially males.

Let us reiterate: if you do not ensure that people with autism are treated as favourably as others in any of the services you provide, you can now be the subject of a legal claim where a person with autism, or their representative, can seek a declaration that they have been discriminated against and awarded compensation for any injury to feelings that has resulted from that discrimination.

The triad of impairments

Social impairments

People with autism	This can lead to	Possible reasonable adjustments
• Can actively avoid eye contact and/or have awkward eye contact.	• Appearing rude, avoiding people and being deliberately antisocial • Missing communications between people • Having difficulties in sharing the same attention of other people • Failing to interpret cues from others • Having difficulties in establishing rapport.	• Remove the dependency on eye contact in a communication • Make interpersonal communications explicit • Check understanding of any communications • Provide a focus during the communication (e.g. visuals, paperwork, etc.) • Allow time to acclimatise to people.
• Find it difficult to gauge what the other person might be feeling in a social interaction and/or not consider that the feelings they know about have a role to play during an interaction.	• Being unable to take account of another person's point of view • Failing to share enjoyment or mood with others • Failing to recognise the emotional state of others • Appearing uncaring or callous • Making naïve comments or interactions • Chronically misunderstanding intentions.	• Make communications and feelings explicit • Ask others to make their point of view explicit in ways that the person with autism will understand • Point out links between external behaviours and internal states of mind where appropriate (e.g. during appraisals or supervisions and tutorials).
• Might not respond in ways that would be expected when they are spoken to.	• Having arguments over behaviours and tasks • Causing stress, confusion and anxiety in others • Behaving in ways that are out of place • Disrupting class, office and many situations.	• Allow time to acclimatise to situations and people • Check levels of understanding of the expectations of task, situation and interaction • Check intended communication of the person with autism and how it relates to the situation or task • Demonstrate what is required • Provide written and visual instructions of expectations.

Table continues

Social impairments cont.

People with autism	This can lead to	Possible reasonable adjustments
May not always see themselves as part of or belonging to the social community or family group.	• Being an outsider and appearing socially aloof • Not automatically taking part in activities • Failing to share the 'mood' with others • Exhibiting out of place behaviours and interactions • Having difficulties in 'bonding' with others • Lacking team spirit.	• Make group roles explicit • Introduce formats for team events or activities.
Have difficulties in reading and using facial expressions.	• Having problems conveying internal states of mind • Miscommunicating intentions • Having difficulties in reading or picking up the intentions and communications of other people through body language • Appearing rude or callous and aloof.	• Use communications not reliant on facial expressions • Make communications explicit • Check understandings.
May not respond to affection, help or support from others May not seek help or support from others.	• Appearing deliberately antisocial • Having problems sharing the same attention of others • Having difficulties establishing rapport • Experiencing family and relationship difficulties • Having misunderstanding about competence • Appearing emotionally detached and uncaring • Having school and work related problems.	• Ensure procedures for asking for help are explicit • Demonstrate how to get help and when • Check levels of understanding and competence • Offer non-judgemental help and support • Inform colleagues and others about autism • Make help and support explicit and gradual.
Can sometimes be excessively polite and/or too formal in relating to other people Can stick rigidly to the rules of a social interaction without the accompanying understanding.	• Not being easily accepted as part of a group • Being off-putting in meetings and social situations • Being bullied in schools or colleges • Experiencing social isolation • Having misunderstandings in dealing with others • Misreading levels of competence.	• Avoid situations where this might become a serious problem • Explain to others about autism • Check levels of understanding.

Social impairments cont.

People with autism	This can lead to	Possible reasonable adjustments
• Exhibit little or no play or engage in abnormal social play activities. • May often prefer solitary activities.	• Not becoming part of a group • Missing out on sharing and taking part • Avoiding social gatherings and situations • Not being part of a team • Having restricted abilities and motivations for some activities and jobs.	• Organise so that the person with autism does not always have to be part of a group • Host the person with autism in a group • Allow time to acclimatise to others, routines and the group or team • Make group and 'play' activities well structured.
• Have (so-called) impaired peer relationships • May lack understanding of how to make friends or the social conventions involved in being with other people.	• Having problems taking part • Experiencing social isolation, bullying and inclusion issues • Having problem behaviours where attempts are made to make friends • Experiencing family and relationship problems.	• Host the person with autism • Create informal but structured situations where people can get to know the person with autism • Allow time to acclimatise to other people • Make introductions • Establish a routine and formal habits of interaction.
• May confuse the reciprocal nature of 'normal' interactions.	• Failing to respond to what is expected • Exhibiting inappropriate behaviours or actions • Interacting regardless of status and relationship • Having difficulties judging levels of interest of other people • Intruding on space or in conversations • Having a variety of social problems.	• Check understanding of expectations • Make explicit the expected nature of interactions between people • Ensure understanding of status and what is considered appropriate • Inform others (colleagues etc.) about autism • Check levels of understanding • Ensure immediate and concrete feedback about performance and required improvements.
• In the main, seem to be in a world of their own.	• Experiencing all the above and… • Not staying up to date with fashions and trends • Following interests that may exclude being with other people • Lacking interest in being with other people • Experiencing family and relationship problems.	• Implement the above • Do not put in positions where the person with autism is expected to be sociable or demands high levels of team work, social interaction and communication.

Table continues

Communication

People with autism	This can lead to	Possible reasonable adjustments
May repeat words spoken to them (this is known as echolalia).	• Being confused during conversation • Experiencing misunderstandings over comprehension • Overestimating verbal competence of the individual • Being very disruptive socially.	• Reduce stress (see Chapter 1) • Allow time to acclimatise • Check levels of understanding • Ensure the person with autism is not bored • Use other forms of communication such as signs and writing.
May explain things or give answers in much greater detail than is necessary.	• Having an appearance of social oddness • Being ostracised from peers • Appearing to have a pedantic nature • Being offputting to others • Being unable to gauge level of interest of listeners.	• Be clear about how much information is needed • Give clear guidance on expectations • Explain to others about autism • Be explicit about required answer.
May have word-finding problems, confusion over meaning of words and the sounds between words.	• Being confused during conversation • Raising questions about the person's levels of comprehension • Raising questions about the person's competence • Misunderstanding words etc.	• Check levels of comprehension • Use written rather than spoken communications.
Can be quite literal in interpreting phrases (e.g. the drinks are on the house or it's raining cats and dogs).	• Making mistakes in carrying out instructions • Misunderstanding communications of others • Misreading expectations.	• Check levels of comprehension • Ensure communications less abstract in language • Use written communications.
May find humour and jokes difficult to grasp.	• Experiencing isolation from peers • Being vulnerable to being taken advantage of • Encountering lack of sharing and joint attention • Misunderstanding social situations.	• Do not make understanding of humour part of task or job description • Explain autism to colleagues and others • Where possible explain the joke.

Communication cont.

People with autism	This can lead to	Possible reasonable adjustments
• May have problems with the volume of their voices and can be too loud or too quiet • May sound mechanical or robotic, their intonation may be odd, and pitch, intonation and stress awkward.	• Experiencing social isolation • Being disruptive in a variety of situations • Raising questions about the person's competence.	• Give immediate feedback if disruption is occurring • Role-play the required levels of intonation if appropriate.
• Find that social communication in the use of body language, gestures, facial expressions, gait, posture or deportment can be misread and misused.	• Being picked upon or bullied • Generating fear or anxiety in others • Raising questions about the person's social competence • Generating concerns over behaviour • Becoming oversensitive to criticism or feedback.	• Explain autism to other people • Demonstrate and give feedback about personal expression (e.g. When you stand like that, people think…) • Deliver feedback cautiously • Offer basic 'lessons' in body language specific to the problem and the person • Do not make deportment issues part of the task • Use other forms of communication (e.g. written).
• May fail to sustain or engage in conversation and may have a limited repertoire of 'conversational' topics • May have difficulties in knowing what is *relevant* to talk about.	• Asking questions repetitively • Having a lack of understanding of abstract concepts • Using irrelevant conversational topics • Being socially isolated.	• Do not expect the person with autism to be a great conversationalist • Do not make 'conversational abilities' part of the task • Reduce anxiety levels.
• May fail to understand suggestions, warnings or teasing.	• Experiencing vulnerabilities • Having frequent misunderstandings • Encountering compliance problems.	• Make explicit what you mean • Use concise language • Use pictorial information • Seek the advice of a speech and language therapist.

Table continues

Imagination

People with autism	This can lead to	Possible reasonable adjustments
• Can lack the facilities for creative play.	• Being ostracised from peers • Not becoming part of team or class easily • Being offputting to others.	• Avoid tasks based around creative play abilities • Demonstrate alternative activities • Do not make creativity part of the task.
• Can have odd and repetitive body movements, such as flicking, twisting, spinning.	• Generating discomfort on the part of others • Having difficulties in engaging in tasks and activities • Miscommunicating.	• Give time to acclimatise • Reduce anxiety if needed • Build repetitive movements into the task.
• May become distressed with what seem trivial changes in their environments.	• Developing problem behaviours • Being unable to take part in lessons or meetings • Having difficulties in task performance • Possibly needing to exit from situation.	• Build their own routine into the one that is expected, where appropriate. • Predict change and makes plans for changes in advance • Present alternatives • Allow time to acclimatise to change.
• Can seem 'unreasonable' in their need to follow a particular routine in detail.	• Constantly checking and needing reassurances • Doing things their own way and being insistent • Experiencing anxieties if unable to perform routine.	• Build their routine into the one that is expected, where appropriate and not too disruptive • Teach use of diaries and notes in order to refer to these rather than having to ask same question over and over • Reduce stress • Do not let routine develop in the first place but establish an appropriate one.
• May have a significantly restricted range of interest or preoccupations with one 'narrow' interest.	• Using repetitive conversation and interactions • Allowing their own interests to dominate • Having difficulties getting off topic and onto work • Being ostracised by peers • Experiencing family and relationship problems.	• Inform others about autism • Check levels of comprehension and understanding in performing tasks • Avoid too much conversation in communications and use alternatives.

Imagination cont.

People with autism	This can lead to	Possible reasonable adjustments
• Can have impairments in their abilities to copy or imitate.	• Failing to respond to some tasks through demonstration • Failing to pick up expectations • Having problems fitting in with teams or groups.	• Do not rely on demonstrations • Make expectations explicit • Give explicit guidance if needed on how to do things.

Table continues

Theory of mind

People with autism	This can lead to	Possible reasonable adjustments
People with autism have impairments in their *theory of mind*, in their ability to think about other people in the 'usual' ways. They find mind-reading difficult. This difficulty is sometimes referred to as 'mind-blindness' and it is linked to problems of 'pretending' and 'representing' (thinking about).	• Having problems in recognising feelings in others.	• Do not make task success dependent on empathetic skills • Make feelings explicit • Do not expect the person to 'get it'.
	• Experiencing difficulties sharing.	• Do not make task success dependent on sharing abilities • Organise turn-taking structures • Make sharing part of routine and habit • Allow person with autism time to acclimatise to other people.
	• Having difficulties conjuring a scenario to think about.	• Do not make 'speculation' part of task • Present information visually • Help sequence thoughts and tasks to an end point.
	• Working out other people's intentions and motives	• Make intentions and motives explicit • Allow time to acclimatise to new people • Form positive working habits and routines around people.
	• Finding it hard to explain and articulate their own behaviours and points of view..	• Do not make self-consciousness part of task success • Do not make self-analysis critical to task • Give immediate non-judgemental feedback • Use visual communications.

This can lead to	Possible reasonable adjustments
• Having problems seeing how their own behaviour affects what people think of them.	• Give immediate non-judgemental feedback • Do not make self-awareness critical to task success • Use cartoons or written information and flow charts.
• Experiencing problems taking into account what it is that other people know.	• Do not make reading other people essential to task success or part of job • Allow time to get to know the person with autism and acclimatise.
• Having difficulties speculating on the likes and dislikes of other people. • Failing to appreciate that other people have different points of view.	• Do not make thinking about other people critical to the task, job or lesson • Other people's likes and dislikes need to be made explicit. • Other people may need to make their points of view explicit • Do not make understanding other people's point of view essential to task.
• Having difficulties in reading what is going on between people in social situations.	• Break down social situation for the person (hosting) • Do not make reading social situations critical to success.
• Generally failing to attribute separate and valid desires that other people have.	• Other people may need to be explicit about their desires and needs • Again do not make reading and understanding other people's desires or needs critical to the task.

Table continues

People with autism	This can lead to	Possible reasonable adjustments
• Put simply *central coherence* is the psychological process by which we make meaning and we are able to see the whole picture (Frith 1989). It is the process by which we take in various types of information, say for example in a story, and we pull the information together to get the *gist*, the general idea; instead of recalling every single detail or just the odd fragment.	• Dealing with or thinking about abstract concepts. • Having problems seeing the bigger picture.	• Avoid abstract concepts • Give concrete explanation of abstract ideas • Provide visual cues. • Do not make seeing the bigger picture part of task • Explain more • Use templates for the person with autism to work with.
	• Attending to detail (which may not be the detail required). • Experiencing difficulties in seeing the *meaning* of various pieces of information. • Failing to make sense of disparate information.	• Make use of the person's abilities to focus on details where appropriate • Avoid giving too much information. • Do not make finding meaning or coherence part of the task • Provide formats for drawing together information. • Manage information for the person • Forms and templates to elicit information may be helpful • Provide plans and schedules, schemes of work.

This can lead to	Possible reasonable adjustments
• Having problems in integrating a variety of different information to form a coherent message.	• As above • Teach use of diaries and notebooks • Do not make trying to integrate information a critical part of any task.
• Not sharing the same focus of attention as others.	• Explicitly point out to the person what needs to be paid attention to and why • Make focal point of meeting very obvious.
• Being unable to always pick out the expected behaviour in a situation by reading the social cues.	• Provide concrete information on the behaviours that are expected in various situations • Do not make social skills essential to task.
• Having problems choosing and deciding on priorities when faced with the need to make decisions.	• Make decision information visual • Provide decision trees • Allow the person with autism time to 'experience' what they are choosing between.
• Experiencing chronic difficulties generalising what is learnt in one situation to another and transferring skills in one task to another.	• Always, always, always teach the skills needed in the situations in which they will occur • Do not assume that skills will be or can be generalised from one task or situation to another. • Demonstrate how existing skills can be transferred
• Finding it difficult to relate to new and novel tasks.	• Allow time to acclimatise • Plan for new tasks to occur • Prepare the person with autism for new task • Get into good habits and routines.

Table continues

Executive functioning

People with autism

- *Executive functioning* is the mental ability we all have to plan actions, organise and respond, monitor and control ourselves, be flexible in our thinking, research and deal with change. Problems with poor executive functioning occur within the normal population and among people with other impairments. However, coupled with problems of communication and what we have seen of the problems related to the theory of mind and central coherence, for people with autism problems related to poor executive functioning are exacerbated.

This can lead to

- Being poorly organised.

- Poor sequencing skills

Possible reasonable adjustments

- Provide timetables
- Allow time to establish routine
- Help to use diaries and plan out sequence of activities
- Do not expect the person with autism to organise themselves or materials.

- Provide templates for sequencing
- Do not expect the person with autism to be able to sequence
- Use real-life prompts for sequence.

This can lead to	*Possible reasonable adjustments*
• Having problems talking about future events.	• Do not make talking about future events essential to the task • Give visual information of the future event • Show final or end product or goal to be achieved • Use concrete language • Always use lesson plans, schemes of work and task schedules • Provide examples of end results.
• Planning a series of events or actions (simple or complex).	• Do not make planning an essential part of the task • Provide templates and formats, e.g. diaries, to aid planning • Allow time to establish routine • Establish habit for planning • Provide lesson plans, schemes of work and task schedules (as above).
• Having difficulty holding on to an idea and thinking about it.	• Do not expect the person with autism to be able to *think about* abstract concepts • Use written communications and concrete language • Provide visual information of topic • Provide lesson plans, schemes of work and task schedules (as above).
• Copying and imitating being impaired.	• Do not only use demonstrations • Physically show person how to do something • Use clear modelling and/or visuals.

Table continues

UNIVERSIT⎯ ⎯⎯HESTER LIBRARY

Executive functioning cont.

This can lead to	Possible reasonable adjustments
• Having difficulty starting and stopping a task.	• Give cues and prompts • Use a stop watch • Making beginnings, middles and ends very obvious and explicit • Ensure students or employees have lesson plans or clear task outlines.
• Lacking inhibition in emotional responses, leading to impulsive behaviours.	• Give non-judgemental feedback • Try to ensure the person with autism has an established routine • Try to ensure that expectations are clear • Provide clear plans and explicit information on what is going to happen (reduce surprise).
• Having problems in planning and using strategies for a task.	• Allow the person with autism to use template for carrying out a task • Allow time to acclimatise • Prepare student for any new tasks in advance • Give modelled examples.
• Experiencing difficulties taking in new information and using it.	• Allow time to acclimatise • Show how information is relevant to the task • Provide information in various formats.
• Being impulsive when carrying out a task or activity.	• Break task down into steps • Ensure the person with autism has listened to or read any instructions carefully • Ensure each step has beginning, middle and end.
• Having a chronic need for things in their place.	• Allow for things to be in their place as far as possible.

Sensitivities and sensing impairments

People with autism	This can lead to	Possible reasonable adjustments
• People with autism and Asperger syndrome can be sensitive to light, touch, noise, etc. and have difficulty integrating sensory information.	• Disliking certain clothes and textiles • Wearing same clothes.	• Allow time to acclimatise to new clothes • Do not underestimate need for sameness.
	• Disliking getting dirty • Being unable to undertake a range of activities (e.g. painting), messy tasks etc.	• Avoid messy activities • Use gloves.
	• Avoiding door handles • Avoiding touching other items.	• Introduce gloves if appropriate • Do not underestimate what appears to be an irrational fear of some objects.
	• Being irritated when exposed to some smells, food stuffs or textiles • Suffering sickness from exposure to smells and so on.	• Avoid certain food stuffs, perfumes, smells etc.
	• Experiencing eating problems • Eating only some foods or the same things • Feeling disgust at eating at all.	• Always seek the advice of a nutritionist • Seek alternative ways of offering or disguising food.
	• Keeping fingers in ears • Blocking out sounds.	• Make the activity not dependent on hearing • Offer headphones (although blocking with fingers may be a way of avoiding using hands) • Reduce noise levels where possible.

Table continues

Sensitivities and sensing impairments cont.

This can lead to

- Avoiding eye contact.

- Disliking or feeling discomfort at being hugged
- Refusing to be touched or have hair washed.

- Disliking open spaces
- Feeling disorientated and confused in open places.

- Experiencing panic in supermarkets, cinemas etc.
- Developing impulsive behaviours and being overstimulated.

- Being unable to process pain or discomfort
- Failing to sense danger or threat.

- Being easily distracted by extraneous noises or sounds
- Being distracted from task by smells (e.g. cooking).

Possible reasonable adjustments

- Do not make eye contact essential to task success
- Remove the need to look *and* listen
- Take the person to see an optician
- Provide sunglasses and/or brimmed hat (even a hoodie!).

- Do not hug the person with autism
- Inform others
- Teach person to say: 'I do not like being touched.'

- Avoid open spaces
- Anchor using bollard (e.g. during sports) so the person knows where to stand
- Ensure the person knows where to go, point out signposts, landmarks etc.
- Use personal radios, earmuffs.

- Avoid supermarkets etc.
- Take time to acclimatise and keep to a set routine in a supermarket
- Use a personal radio and sunglasses to cut down stimulation
- Make plans and prepare beforehand using photos etc.

- One-to-one support in potential hazardous areas.

- Provide headphones.
- Make environmental changes

This can lead to

- Having problems processing and distinguishing different sounds
- Making blocking noises (e.g. humming, singing constantly).
- Needing to have everything in its place. (Related to executive functioning and central coherence)
- Being unable to cope if small items are moved or displaced.
- Developing touching behaviours (e.g. very short hair, walls).

- Being unable to enter crowded room or place
- Failing to use public transport
- Feeling disorientated in crowded places or classrooms etc.

Possible reasonable adjustments

- Practice in situ may help
- Decrease environmental stimulation.
- Allow for things to be in place
- Plan for changes
- Prepare the person with autism for need for moving things.
- Planning and preparation
- Friendly hint or reminder from a colleague of consequences.
- Seek out alternatives to the crowded room if possible
- Provide lots of preparation and planning
- Provide alternatives to public transport if possible cycles, moped etc.
- Structure any visits as far as possible
- Get into the habit of going out in order to acclimatise.

5

If You Have Been Discriminated Against

Nicholas Graham

Introduction

If you consider that you have been discriminated against, then whether you can seek legal redress will depend on who has discriminated against you. Set out below are the options open to anyone contemplating litigation. First, a word of warning: the legal world is an expensive place if you engage professionals to do it on your behalf. The Equality and Human Rights Commission can provide legal assistance in certain cases, but not all. You may want to check if you have any form of legal expenses insurance covered by your household or car insurance policy. You may also want to consider alternatives to litigation, which are set out below.

County court

For claims against colleges of further or higher education, or claims of discrimination against a body providing goods and services, then the appropriate route is through the county court. County court procedures are detailed and are known as the *Civil Procedure Rules*.

Timing

All litigation is subject to time limits. In general the time limit for bringing a claim in the county court is six months from the date the discrimination occurred. Time for issuing a claim can be extended in certain circumstances, but only in exceptional cases. The best advice is to try to get your claim issued as soon as possible.

Pleadings

Again, in common with most litigation, you need to set out your case in writing. If you are bringing the claim then you are called the *claimant* and you have to complete a *claim form* together with a statement of case. The *statement of case* should contain brief details of what the claim is about. It usually follows a chronological order – 'Mr X went into the shop on 4 July 2005 to purchase…' – and is written in numbered paragraphs. It is not supposed to contain all the evidence, but rather enough facts to demonstrate to a judge in summary what the claim is about and why there is a *cause of action*, that is, why it is a claim that the court can adjudicate on. After recounting what has happened, you conclude by claiming discrimination contrary to a specific section of the DDA and also set out that damages are claimed, together with interest. It is for the court to assess what those damages are, so you do not need to put in a figure.

All pleadings (documents sent to the court) must have a *statement of truth*, which is a form of words that confirms that you are telling the truth about what you have put in the claim form or statement of case.

In response to a claim form and statement of case, a *defendant* has 28 days from when they receive these documents to file a *defence*. This follows a similar format to the statement of case and normally either agrees with the facts, or disputes them and puts forward the basis of why the claim is disputed or, more rarely, admitted. It is possible to admit the claim in full (admit liability), and then the argument is about what is the appropriate amount of *damages* (sometimes called *quantum*).

After completing the claim form and statement of case and when the defendant sends in their defence, the court will send out *allocation question-naires*. This is a form with a series of questions that enables the court to understand how the case should be prepared for trial. You will need to answers questions such as what are the costs incurred by the parties to date, and how much are likely to be incurred to trial; are there any orders that could be made by the court; what witnesses are needed and have they any dates to avoid?

The court will also ask what *track* is appropriate. Claims are run on the small claims, fast track or multi-track, depending on the value of them. Most DDA cases will be small claims or fast track cases. The significance of that is the type of directions that might be appropriate for preparation for trial.

Directions

In order to manage the case to trial, the court issues *directions*. These are usually agreed between the parties, or decided upon by the court at a case management conference – basically a hearing before a judge.

The normal directions issued are as follows. *Disclosure of documents* which are relevant to the claim: this is normally done by exchanging a list of documents containing all those documents that the parties are prepared to show the other. For those documents that the parties are not able or prepared to disclose, then reasons must be given. If those reasons are not justified, an application for an order for specific disclosure can be made.

Inspection of documents: this involves getting copies of document in the exchanged lists from the other party which the other party has not seen.

Experts: if expert evidence is required – which might involve medical expert evidence about Autistic Spectrum Disorders – then there should be a specific direction about that. You might want to try to get your defendant to admit that you have Autistic Spectrum Disorder so you will not need to go to the trouble of getting a medical opinion about the diagnosis. However, you might still want to get a medical view about the effect of the disability on your ability to carry out normal day-to-day activities.

The defendant might want you to be examined by their own medical practitioner. Sometimes medical experts meet to decide what they can agree and what they disagree on.

The other normal direction is for the exchange of *witness statements*. This is the parties' opportunity to set out in as much detail as they can their side of events, their story about what happened, how it made them feel, why they felt it was discriminatory, or, if you are the defendant, why it was not discriminatory. Witness statements must be written chronologically, with numbered paragraphs and paginated, and also must contain a statement of truth. Witnesses should be asked to come; if they refuse then they can be summoned to attend if an application for a witness summons is applied for.

After these directions have been complied with, it is usual for *listing questionnaires* to be filed with court. These contain specific questions about what will happen at trial, for example how long people will get to ask question, and practical arrangements about the bundle of documents.

The trial

Normally, the trial is in open court and before a judge. The claimant will go first to establish his or her claim. This can involve reading out the witness statement – or the judge may consider that that is not necessary and move straight to questioning. Evidence is given under oath. The judge and the other party have an opportunity to ask questions. Questions from the opponent are known as *cross-examination* in contrast to *examination in chief*, which is questions from your own representative. *Re-examination* is questions from your own representative after cross-examination and should be confined only to new information that arises out of cross-examination.

The decision or judgement

After hearing all the evidence and submissions about the law, the judge makes his/her decision that should cover all the issues and determine any disputes about the facts.

Compensation

The advantage to a claimant of going to the county court is that it can award compensation if a finding is made that discrimination has occurred. Compensation is not very large, however. The sorts of awards for injury to feelings range anywhere between £5000 on the lower end to £15,000 at the upper end. More can be awarded for grosser forms of discrimination.

Costs

The disadvantage of dealing with a claim in the county court is the risk that, if you lose, the other party will claim costs against you. As a judge commented in a recent decision, English law requires that those who seek a remedy must risk paying for it if they lose. Costs can be large if solicitors are engaged and barristers are used at the hearing.

Employment Tribunal

Employment tribunals follow a similar procedure to the county court, although the rules of procedure are much less strict. There are still time limits for bringing a claim. A *complaint* (the equivalent of the claim form and statement of case in the county court) has to be lodged with the Tribunal within six months from the date when discrimination occurred. This is done by completing a form ET1, which is produced by the Tribunal Service, giving details of pay, years of service, the name of the employer etc. There is also space to fill out the details of the complaint. Again, as with statements of case, this should not be all the evidence, but a summary of basic facts which enables the Tribunal to know that there is a case that they can properly consider.

When lodged, the Tribunal Service sends a copy to the employer (the *respondent*) who has 28 days to lodge a *response* on a form called an ET3.

You can also send a *questionnaire* to your employer asking questions that might elicit more information about discriminatory practices or policies. If your employer fails to respond to the questionnaire within a reasonable time then the Tribunal can draw adverse inferences from the failure to respond – that is they are more likely to say that an employer has acted unreasonably and possible unlawfully.

Once the complaint and response are with the Tribunal then there is a *conciliation period* when the Advisory Conciliation and Arbitration Service (ACAS) may contact both parties with a view to seeing if there is any scope for settlement. If there is, normally the ACAS officer will attempt to broker that deal and get the parties to sign an agreement (known as a *COT 3*). That brings the proceedings to a stop. If a settlement is not possible within the conciliation period, then the parties are free to continue to attempt settlement, but would do that between themselves.

The Tribunal will then issue *directions* – again, as in the county court – those directions include: agreeing the document bundle and exchange of witness statements. Tribunals also like you to provide details of losses, that is how much you have lost because you have been discriminated against. If you have been dismissed then the losses would include loss of pay; if you complain about other forms of discrimination then you can receive compensation for injury to feelings.

Witnesses can be asked to come, and like in the county court you can ask for a witness to be ordered to attend if they can give relevant evidence. You will need to ask the Tribunal to issue a summons to that witness.

At a hearing the procedure is much like a formal court hearing, with the parties taking turns to give their evidence and be questioned about what they say. Witnesses swear an oath or affirm that they are telling the truth.

The Tribunal is usually more proactive in asking questions and they are usually more relaxed about the admission of evidence which a county court might exclude if, for example, it was served late.

At the conclusion of the hearing the Tribunal will give its decision or send the parties a written decision. If you have won, the Tribunal will then assess the level of compensation payable to you.

Special Educational Needs and Disability Tribunal

A claim that a school has discriminated against a pupil who has disabilities will be heard in the Special Educational Needs and Disability Tribunal (SENDIST). The procedure that is followed by the SENDIST is different again from an employment tribunal and the county court.

The type of claim that SENDIST hear can be anything that concerns the provision of education to a pupil, for example fixed term exclusions, refusing to allow a child to go on a school trip, not allowing a child to participate in an activity; indeed, as indicated in Chapter 2, any justifiable sense of grievance that might arise out of a decision the school may take. (Permanent exclusions, however, are dealt with by an independent appeal panel – see below.) Similarly, claims against local authorities can be made where the complaint is about the exercise of a function by that local authority.

As with all forms of litigation however, time limits do apply and a claim must be brought within six months of when the discrimination occurred (slightly extended in limited circumstances).

There is a prescribed form available from the SENDIST website (www.sendist.gov.uk, accessed 27.11.07) which is known as a *notice of claim*. The notice of claim requires information about you as parents and the school or local authority, if they have discriminated against your child.

The notice of claim is then served on the local authority, which has 30 days to respond with what is known as the *case statement*. The parents can also have that time period to respond with their case statement if they want to.

Your case statement elaborates on the notice of claim, providing further details as to why you say your child has a disability and has been discriminated against. The local authority's case statement will cover the response to your submission outlining why it defends the claim, why it is not discrimination, or why it thinks reasonable adjustments have been made, or cannot be made or why its treatment is justified.

Once all that information has been lodged with the Tribunal, the SENDIST undertakes to paginate the documents and will list the matter for a hearing date. The paginated index bundle is then sent to the parties.

It is not uncommon for there to be the filing of late evidence which may include reports that were not available at the time the case statement was due to be filed. Late evidence is admissible in certain circumstances principally, where it is in the interest of the child, a copy has been served on the other party and could not reasonably be available at the time the case statement was filed.

Witnesses can be ordered to attend by the SENDIST. They do not normally come with any witness statement, as usually the witness is either the head teacher of the school which the child is already attending or the officer responsible for making the decision that has been complained about.

Witnesses who do not attend can provide witness statements. If their evidence is contested then the Tribunal may put less weight on the evidence in the witness statement than oral evidence given by someone who attends the Tribunal.

The Tribunal is much more informal than either an employment tribunal or a court. There is no formal oath taking and the Tribunal generally takes the lead in terms of questioning the witnesses, the local authority officers and the parents.

Once the SENDIST has considered all the evidence it will normally send a written decision to the parties some 14 days after the hearing. A party can request a review of that decision if it is in the interest of justice and there will sometimes be a further hearing to consider that review.

An appeal can be made from the Tribunal to the High Court only on a point of law. The remedy in SENDISTs are limited.

Independent appeal panels for school exclusions

Independent appeal panels deal with claims for disability discrimination in relation to permanent exclusion. The process for excluding a child permanently from school starts with a decision by the head teacher, who must comply with the Department for Children, Schools and Families guidance when making a decision to exclude and that guidance sets out what the procedure requires. This involves an appeal to the governing body of the school. If the decision of the governing body is to uphold the head teacher's decision then you have a right for a further appeal to the independent appeal panel.

There is a clerk to the independent appeal panel (IAP) whose role is to collate all the necessary evidence and arrange the hearing and ensure that you and the school have all available material for the hearing. The hearing is before three panel members and usually follows an informal procedure with a set agenda.

A recent case known as R (T) v. IAP of Devon County Council [2007] EWHC 763 (admin) in the High Court set out the questions that the independent appeal panel should address when considering whether a child has been discriminated against.

First, the IAP should consider whether the child is disabled within the meaning of the DDA. Second, the IAP should consider whether the school has treated the child less favourably. In most cases the obvious answer to this will be Yes, given that a child whose behaviour was normal would unlikely to be faced with an exclusion – remember, less favourable treatment has to be compared with somebody without a disability.

The third question is whether exclusion arose for a reason which related to the pupil's disability. In many circumstances this may be quite a difficult question to answer. You will no doubt put forward the case that it was the child's disability that meant that he or she acted in a particular way. A school may consider that the behaviour was simply naughtiness rather than any particular disability.

The fourth question to address is whether the less favourable treatment was material to the circumstances of the case and substantial. In looking at that question the school is going to be given some latitude in making appropriate management decisions where, for example, teachers have to manage the behaviour of a child who is particularly disruptive.

The fifth question is whether the school had failed to make any reasonable adjustments and if the answer to that was that the school *had* failed to make reasonable adjustments then the question is would the less favourable treatment have been justified even if the school had made reasonable adjustments. Again, this is a difficult area. If, for example, a child's Asperger syndrome meant that the child's behaviour was difficult at school, which resulted in exclusion, and the school could have made various reasonable adjustments at an earlier stage in the pupil's school career, then it would be hard pressed to justify the exclusion, unless of course it could show that the exclusion would have been justified even if the reasonable adjustments had been undertaken.

The panel will hear all the evidence and give the parties an opportunity to say what they wish or ask their own questions. A decision will be made quickly – usually the same day – and a letter sent out to you with the reasons for the decision.

Mediation

Fortunately there are alternatives to litigation. The most common alternative, and one encouraged by the courts more and more, is mediation. Mediation is a process usually involving an independent mediator who seeks to bring both sides of the dispute together and work out a resolution to their dispute which is acceptable to both parties.

The first stage is usually finding and appointing a mediator. There are a variety of providers, who charge various fees. You might be able to persuade your opponent to pay the mediator's costs in full, or agree to split the fees.

Unlike the court, which imposes the process on the parties to a dispute, the mediation process is a matter for agreement. You can agree which documents you think would be helpful to the dispute; in much mediation the parties draft out what might be called a position statement: a non-technical document which describes what the dispute is about and what things are important to you. It can also set out what remedy you are looking for as your ideal solution. That could be anything from an apology, a job reference, compensation, a better working relationship, reinstatement into school – often more complicated and subtle settlements than could be achieved by going to court or to a tribunal.

Normally, although not always, the parties meet with the mediator present. They may start off in an open forum with you setting out what you want to achieve by the mediation – setting out your best case. After that, the parties will retire to separate rooms and the mediator will often shuttle between the two rooms: discussing the case, making proposals, outlining options, conveying to the other side where there is agreement, testing arguments, speculating as to what might happen if agreement is not reached. All this is with a view to enabling the parties to get to a position that they are both prepared to accept or live with as an outcome.

If an agreement cannot be reached then nothing is lost – other than the time spent on the mediation, and the fees for the mediator. The whole event is 'without prejudice' to any future court proceedings, which means that you cannot raise in court at a future date issues discussed at the mediation, such as the offers or admissions that the other side made to you. If you have a successful mediation, then an agreement is drawn up which sets out the terms of the agreement. This is a binding agreement that acts like a contract between the parties.

In litigation there are winners and losers. The losers have to pay for their risk in seeking a remedy in the courts that includes paying the winning side's costs. If you go to tribunal, although you might not have to pay your opponents' costs you might have to pay a lawyer to assist you through the process. In mediation, your costs risk is low and there is a very real possibility that you will come out satisfied that your grievance has been considered by the other side in detail; you will learn something about your opponent; you may even come out of the mediation with exactly what you wanted without the other side thinking that they have lost.

Often in the employment situation or with schools, you want the relationship to continue even if you consider that discrimination has occurred. Mediation is an excellent way of having the dispute addressed, and maintaining the relationship throughout the process.

UNIVERSITY OF WINCHESTER
LIBRARY

Conclusion

By way of conclusion we offer a summary. In Chapter 1 we have looked at an overview of the impairments of autism:

- *Triad of impairment*: the triad comprises social interaction (difficulty with relationships and interacting), communication (difficulty with verbal and non-verbal communication) and imagination (difficulty in the ability to 'think about' things).

- *Theory of mind*: people with autism have impairments in their theory of mind, in their ability to think about other people in the 'usual' ways. They find mind-reading difficult. This difficulty is sometimes referred to as 'mind-blindness' and it is linked to problems of 'pretending' and 'representing' (thinking about).

- *Central coherence*: this is the psychological process by which we make meaning and we are able to see the whole picture. It is the process by which we take in various types of information, say for example in a story, and we pull the information together to get the *gist*, the general idea, instead of recalling every single detail or just the odd fragment.

- *Executive functioning*: this is the mental ability we all have to plan actions, organise and respond, monitor and control ourselves, be flexible in our thinking, research and deal with change.

We also looked very briefly at the fact that some people with autism and Asperger syndrome can be sensitive to light, touch, noise, etc. and have difficulty integrating sensory information.

In Chapter 2 we looked at the Disability Discrimination Act 1995. We saw that – if it was not already obvious – certain types of autism fall well within the definition of a 'disability' given the long-term and adverse effect that autism has on normal day-to-day activities. We also noted that proving a disability was one thing, but demonstrating that you had been discriminated against on the grounds of your disability was quite another. But the law is clear: there is now a legal requirement to ensure that those with autism are not treated less favourably as compared to others, unless it can be shown that such treatment was justified. We also looked at the additional duty to make reasonable adjustments to address the disadvantage that this form of disability creates, an obligation unique to discrimination law and one that calls for some thought and creativity on the part of the employer, school or service provider.

In Chapter 3 we looked at what these legal requirements to make reasonable adjustments for people with autism might look like through a series of case studies.

One of the purposes of this chapter was to show how in some cases the behaviours of people with autism can be seen by others as 'anti-social', 'silly', 'offensive' or 'naughty', but what we hope to have shown is how these behaviours may arise as a direct result of adaptations and adjustments *not* being in place *and* from the person being treated less favourably in comparison with other people without autism. The behaviours arise from being discriminated against.

In chapter 4 we provided a *guide* to common behaviours, how they relate to the impairment of autism and what reasonable adjustments could be made. This list is meant as reference guide and is by no means exhaustive or meant to be definitive.

It is our view that the industry of support services, university courses, books and research groups that has grown up around the emergence of people with autism needs to shift from looking at ways that they 'should' help people with autism fit in and be included to what legal duties they 'must' adhere to.

It is no longer enough to try to persuade individuals with autism that it is they who need to change by teaching them general 'social skills' – the very things in which they are impaired. It is no longer enough to write on a statement of special educational needs that a person with autism has 'problems concentrating in class' or 'poor relationships with peers' and needs to be taught how to concentrate or have his or her social skills improved – the school must make reasonable adjustments. It is no longer right that people with autism should be told that they will be able to learn things and do things that they do not have the facilities for. Nor is it right that people with autism need to develop or learn 'coping strategies' – over and above those that all of us need.

Finally, it is no longer right that people with autism are excluded from schools, colleges, services and employment simply because they have autism.

Author Biographies

James Graham

James worked for many years at a senior level for the UK's National Autistic Society. He was then Principal of The INTERACT Centre, a grade one further education college in London for people with Asperger syndrome. He is now an independent consultant and has worked and provided training and consultation for careers services, regional Learning and Skills Councils, national charities, private care homes, local education authorities, social services and further education colleges. He is also a regular speaker at national conferences.

Nicholas Graham – author of Chapters 2 and 5

Nicholas Graham, LLB (Hons), Solicitor, is Assistant Head of Legal Services at Oxfordshire County Council and principal adviser on education and disability issues. He has worked in local government since 1997 and is lead professional for the Solicitors in Local Government Group of the Law Society and is secretary to the Education Special Interest Group for the London and Home Counties Branch of the Solicitors in Local Government Group. He is also Chair of Governors for Grandpont Nursery School and Children's Centre in Oxford.

References

American Psychiatric Association (1994) *Diagnostic and Statistical Manual of Mental Disorders*, 4th edn (DSM-IV). Washington, DC: American Psychiatric Association.

Asperger, H. (1944) 'Autistic Psychopathy in Childhood.' Translated and annotated by U. Frith in U. Frith (ed.) (1991) *Autism and Asperger Syndrome.* Cambridge: Cambridge University Press.

Baird, G., Simonoff, E., Pickles, A., Chandler, S., Loucas, T. *et al.* (2006). 'Prevalence of disorders of the autism spectrum in a population cohort of children in South Thames: The Special Needs and Autism Project (SNAP).' *The Lancet 368*, 9531, 179–181.

Barnes, C., Oliver, M. and Barton, L. (eds) (2002) *Disability Studies Today.* Cambridge: Polity Press.

BBC (2006) 'Schools "fail autistic children".' *CBBC Newsround*, 16 September. Available at www.bbc.co.uk (accessed 27.11.07).

Bridger, B.M. (2006) 'Council's "appalling" treatment of autistic worker in landmark case.' *Ealing Times*, 16 February.

Cumine, V., Leach, J. and Stevenson, G. (1998) *Asperger Syndrome: A Practical Guide for Teachers.* London: David Fulton.

Disability Rights Commission (2002) *Disability Discrimination Act 1995, Code of Practice. Rights of Access. Goods, Facilities, Services and Premises.* Available at www.nads.org.uk/documents/DRC_code_of_practice.pdf (accessed 27.11.07).

Disability Rights Commission (2007) *Code of Practice (revised) for Providers of Post-16 Education and Related Services.* Available at www.equalityhuman-rights.com (accessed 27.11.07).

Fitzgerald, M. (2006) *Autism, Asperger's Syndrome and Creativity.* Available at www.awares.org/conferences (accessed 27.11.07).

Frith, U. (1989) *Autism: Explaining the Enigma.* Oxford: Blackwell.

Green, H. *et al.* (2005) *Mental Health of Children and Young People in Great Britain, 2004.* Basingstoke: Palgrave Macmillan.

Happé, F. (1994) *Autism: An Introduction to Psychological Theory.* London: UCL Press.

Harris, P. (1995) 'Pretending and Planning.' In S. Baron-Cohen, H. Tager-Flusberg and D.J. Cohen (eds) *Understanding Other Minds: Perspectives from Autism.* Oxford: Oxford University Press.

Howlin, P. (1997) *Autism: Preparing for Adulthood.* London: Routledge.

Howlin, P., Baron-Cohen, S. and Hadwin, J. (1999) *Teaching Children with Autism to Mind-Read.* Chichester: Wiley.

Jordan, R. and Powell, S. (1995) *Understanding and Teaching Children with Autism.* Chichester: Wiley.

Kanner, L. (1943) 'Autistic Disturbances of Affective Contact.' In U. Frith (1989) *Explaining the Enigma.* Oxford: Blackwell.

National Autistic Society (2004) *The Undiscovered Work Force.* London: NAS.

National Autistic Society (2007) *Approaches to Autism.* London: NAS.

Office of Public Sector Information (OPSI) (1995) *Disability Discrimination Act.* London: HMSO, Crown Copyright. Available at www.opsi.gov.uk/acts/acts1995/1995050.htm (accessed 27.11.07).

Ofsted (2004) *Special Educational Needs and Disability: Towards Inclusive Schools,* HMI 2276. London: Ofsted.

Oliver, M. (1990) *The Politics of Disablement.* London: Macmillan.

Perkins, D. (2007) 'Learning disabilities: Are organisations really open to employing staff with learning disabilities?' *Personnel Today,* 29 May. Available at www.PersonnelToday.com (accessed 27.11.07).

Russell, J., Mauthner, N., Sharpe, S. and Tideswell, T. (1991) 'The "windows" task as a measure of strategic deception in preschoolers and autisitc subjects.' *British Journal of Developmental Psychology,* 33 31–3349.

Schuler, A.L., Peck, C.A., Willard, C. and Theimer, K. (1989) 'Assessment of communcative means and function through interviews: Assessing the communicative capabilities of individuals with limited language.' *Seminars in Speech and Language 10,* 51–61.

Smith, A. (2006) 'Teachers struggling with special needs provision, report finds.' *Guardian,* 16 May 2006.

Wing, L. (1981) 'Language, social and cognitive impairments in autism and sever mental retardation.' *Journal of Autism and Developmental Disorders 11,* 31–44.

Wing, L. and Gould, J. (1979) 'Severe impairments of social interaction and associated abnormalities in children: Epidemiology and classification.' *Journal of Autism and Developmental Disorders 9,* 11–29.

World Health Organization (1992) *International Statistical Classification of Diseases and Related Health Problems,* 10th revision (ICD-10). Geneva: WHO.

Index

UNIVERSITY ᴼᶠ ᴹᴬᴺᶜᴴᴱˢTER
LIBRARY